S0-BJH-134

THE TUDOR INTERLUDE

THE TUDOR INTERLUDE
Stage, Costume, and Acting

by

T. W. CRAIK, M.A., Ph.D.

Lecturer in English in the
University of Leicester

LEICESTER
UNIVERSITY PRESS
1962

Made and printed by litho-offset in Great Britain by
William Clowes and Sons, Limited, London and Beccles, for the
Leicester University Press

First impression 1958
Second impression 1962

TO

MY FATHER AND MOTHER

FOREWORD

"KNOW that the life of these things consists in action," John Webster said of his own play. Yet so ephemeral is that moment of embodied life upon the boards that no effort of imaginative sympathy alone can fill out words written four hundred years ago with the power of the *dromenon*, the thing done. The quality of such a play, as it first lived, must be recreated from all the data by scholarly insight, before an act of sympathy can reclothe the lines with the depth of colour, movement, and vivacity that they ought to convey. This, like the art of giving perspective to a picture, is a learned skill.

It is only within the last dozen years that the Elizabethan scaffoldage has been explored as acting-space; that the participation of the audience has been grasped, so that the traffic of the stage is felt as lively interplay between actors and spectators. Perhaps this understanding has been possible simply because in the living theatre there has been a growth of something resembling older habits. The work of such students as Richard Southern and C. Walter Hodges has been linked with theatrical experiment at Bristol and the Mermaid Theatre. Medieval drama, too, in revival which has not attempted to reproduce exactly the old conditions, but to make full use of the knowledge acquired, has proved its power; the Mystery Plays drew crowds to York and Chester and Sir David Lyndsay's *Satyre of the Thrie Estaitis* captivated audiences in Edinburgh.

By his study of the Tudor Interlude, Dr Craik has done much to recover the theatrical tradition of the vital transitional years between medieval and Elizabethan drama. Whether given within the hall or upon the "place," these plays, formerly considered so uncouth, have revealed a dramatic life far deeper than has been suspected. By direct inclusion of the audience, by clowning and fighting, songs and fireworks, false noses and donkeys on wheels, or by the incorporation of convenient dramatic objects, such as the great hearth and the screen doors, the authors have done more than pull out all the stops for entertainment. They have reinforced what they wished to say, and that, in the case of such a writer as William Wager, is something well worth attention.

The Tudor Interlude has the double interest of being itself a vigorous dramatic form, and of providing a basis for the greater works of dramatic poetry which followed. For example, Dr Craik has shown how inevitably a change of garments signifies a change of life, and how powerful are its moral implications in plays where the hero sins, repents, and is reformed. Such a tradition lies behind those great moments when Prince Hal first appears in armour, when Pericles calls for fresh garments, when Cordelia reclothes Lear in royalty. Kent in the stocks again re-enacts a scene well known from the Interludes. Even in the supreme Elizabethan drama, strength is drawn from these familiar roots.

M. C. BRADBROOK

CONTENTS

ILLUSTRATIONS

Between pages 48 and 49

PLATE I. THE LAST JUDGEMENT

Bodleian Library, Oxford (Douce Collection), 133 (387).
Unidentified German woodcut of 1530–40 (school of Cranach).

A grotesque beaked Devil accuses Adam and Eve before the Trinity. Justice and Truth (standing on right) appear for the prosecution, Mercy and Peace (kneeling on left) for the defence. They wear contemporary costume and are without wings, and each has an appropriate and traditional symbol. God the Father has the robes, crown, orb, and sceptre of a king. Christ and especially the Holy Ghost are conventionally represented.

PLATES II AND III. THE PRODIGAL GIVING A BANQUET

Max Geisberg, *Der Deutsche Einblatt-Holzschnitt*, Munich, 1930, No. 350–51.
Reproduction of a woodcut by Jörg Breu the Elder, accompanying a version, in German couplets, of the parable of the prodigal (see Luke, xv, 11–32).

Bodleian Library, Oxford (Douce Collection), W.2.2b (2).

Copy in reverse, by an unidentified (Flemish?) engraver, with the names of characters in *Acolastus* (1529, a Latin "prodigal" play), cards and dice added, and costumes altered to include feathers in the hats of the prodigal Acolastus and Pamphagus, and a fool's cap for Pantolabus (described as *parasitus* in the *dramatis personae* of the play).

PLATE IV. THE PRODIGAL EATING HUSKS

Bodleian Library, Oxford (Douce Collection), W.2.2a (136).
Cornelis Anthonisz (Teunisson)? *Allegory on the Prodigal Son* (one of a series of six woodcuts: Wouter Nighoff, *Nederlandsche Houtsneden*, The Hague, 1933–36, Pl. 189).

The Prodigal has a fool's cap and bells, feeds from a trough inscribed "The Leaven of the Pharisees" (see Matthew, xvi, 5–12), and is accompanied by the soldier War, the lean and ragged Famine, the invalid Sickness (note the kerchief, crutch, and urine bottle), and Despair who has a snake in her bosom ("Gnawing Conscience") and a sword at her heart. God's Vengeance overhangs him, and Death, Hell, and the Devil prepare to make him their prey.

PLATE V. JUSTICE IN THE STOCKS

British Museum, Department of Prints and Drawings, E.8.–151.
Detail from a large woodcut by Peter Flettner, 1525, reproduced in full by Max Geisberg, *Der Deutsche Einblatt-Holzschnitt*, Munich, 1930, No. 813, and described by Campbell Dodgson, *Catalogue of Early German and Flemish Woodcuts, British Museum*, I, 358).
The whole picture shows Usury, Tyranny, Hypocrisy, and Worldly Reason exploiting and deluding the Common People and preventing access to Justice and to God's Word, who appears on the right of the detail, carrying a Bible and wearing the armour of the righteous (see Ephesians vi). Justice has her scales and sword.

PLATE VI. THE DEATH OF THE ENVIOUS MAN

British Museum Library, press-mark C. 37. d. 2.
Woodcut from Stephen Batman's *A christall glasse of Christian reformation*, 1569, H. i.

The good man is plainly dressed; the evildoer wears a tall hat with a feather, and his doublet and breeches are elaborately slashed.

PLATE VII. USURY MOUNTED ON AN ELEPHANT

British Museum Library, press-mark C. 37. d. 2.
Woodcut from Stephen Batman's *A christall glasse of Christian reformation*, 1569, B. iv.

Usury carries several purses in each hand, and a coffer under each arm; other purses hang at his girdle, and a third coffer at his back. The serpent emerging from his bosom indicates malice. His attendant Niggardship appropriately wears a padlocked pouch and has another padlock hanging decoratively at his neck.

PLATE VIII. A PROPHET, A FRIAR, AND A MURDERER

British Museum Library, press-mark C. 37. d. 2.
Woodcut from Stephen Batman's *A christall glasse of Christian reformation*, 1569, C. iv. *verso*.

The prophet's dress is archaic and dignified. Murder, who is perhaps intended to represent a "ruffler," wears a feathered hat and has long false sleeves tucked into his belt at the back, whereas Peace (*i.e.*, a peaceful man) is plainly dressed.

PLATE IX. A PHILOSOPHER

British Museum Library, press-mark C. 34. f. 17.
Woodcut from Stephen Batman's *The trauayled Pylgrime, bringing newes from all partes of the worlde, such like scarce harde of before*, 1569, B. i. *verso*.

Reason is represented as a philosopher, and given dignity by his long beard and flowing robe; the book in his hand symbolizes learning.

PLATE X. A SATIRE ON GLUTTONY, PRIDE, AND COVETOUSNESS

British Museum Library, press-mark C. 57. c. 8.
Woodcut from Stephen Batman's *The new arival of the three Gracis into Anglia*, 1573, F. i. *verso*.

The woodcut is introduced as follows, F.i.: "This picture following on the other side of the leafe, was made by Namtab [*i.e.*, Batman] a Saxon, in Anno 3751 [*i.e.*, 1573], against the abuse of that present time." Particular marks of extravagance in the costume are the wide stuffed breeches, the slashed doublet, and the ribboned hose.

PLATE XI. THE TRIUMPH OF PECUNIA

Bodleian Library, Oxford (Douce Collection), 142 (220).
By Ph. Galle, 1563.

The Latin distich may be rendered: "Deadly Peril and anxious Fear, yoked together in thy chariot, lead thee, O Queen Money. But because thou dost cloak Folly, Theft, and bloody Murder, therefore the strong hope of all these rests in thee." Pecunia rides in a chariot, and her triumphal progress is accompanied by Envy and Pandemia (*i.e.*, All the People: Greek *Pandemos*), besides the allegorical figures named in the distich. Pecunia's cloaking of Latrocinium (robbery with violence) illustrates the relationship between metaphor and action so often seen in the interludes. Her costume, like that of Money in *Liberality and Prodigality*, and *All for Money*, is decorated with coins.

PLATE XII. THE TITLE PAGE OF AN INTERLUDE, SHOWING DETAILED INSTRUCTIONS FOR THE DOUBLING OF PARTS

British Museum Library, press-mark C. 34. d. 56.
Title-page (A. i) of Thomas Preston's *Cambises*, printed by John Allde, n.d. (1570?). Thirty-eight characters are to be played by eight actors. Only characters of women and children are assigned to the last two actors, so that the play could be acted by a company of six grown men and two youths or boys, though of course a boys' company might equally well perform all the characters.

QUOTATIONS AND REFERENCES

QUOTATIONS are from the text of the editions first listed in the bibliography. I have preserved the original spelling except where I have silently corrected such obvious errors as misprinted, reversed, omitted, or duplicated letters (which there seemed to be no value in reproducing), and where I have expanded recognized contractions (printing "hande" instead of "hāde", for example), in order to help the printer and the reader. I have also followed the original punctuation except on the very few occasions when it is positively misleading.

It will be found that most of my quotations from interludes are unsupported by page- or line-references. This is the result not of carelessness but of policy. Most interludes are short, and quotations from them will be easily found (I have tried, where possible, to make the context obvious). They are not divided into acts and scenes, the line-numbering varies from one modern edition to another, and to give page-references to the original editions would help only readers using those editions, or facsimiles, or facsimile reprints like those of the Malone Society. Parenthetical references after all quotations, moreover, would interrupt the reader and profit him very little, and constant direction to end-notes would be a worse distraction.

I have therefore used the end-notes, for the most part, in order to develop points which I could not develop in the text without spoiling continuity, and in order to cite references to books other than interludes. Again with the object of preserving continuity, the numbers directing the reader to the end-notes have generally been placed at the ends (not in the middles) of paragraphs, and the reader will therefore find under each note the references to all the material used in the paragraph to which it belongs.

INTRODUCTION

MY object in this book is to exhibit the Tudor interludes as plays written to be performed, and to suggest that their merits cannot be fully appreciated without examining the kind of performance that they received. (I am not attempting here a complete assessment of their qualities, and shall discuss their topical subjects and their literary styles only when these are directly related to their representation as stage-plays.) That there is abundant theatrical life in plays by John Heywood, Nicholas Udall, and Sir David Lyndsay has always been recognized, but it is not yet commonly recognized that there were many other capable writers of interludes. I am using the term "interlude" in the elastic sense which it was given in the Tudor period. Definitions which restrict the term to farces or amusing disputations like Heywood's do not take account of the fact that Tudor plays called interludes by their authors and publishers normally employ allegorical methods to a didactic purpose; and yet to call such plays moralities creates an artificial distinction between them and the comic plays. My emphasis will, indeed, be upon the "moral interludes," particularly those neglected plays of Elizabeth's reign, rather than on the comedies, which have had their due, and about which little new remains to be said.

The difficulty of defining Tudor plays is the result merely of a period during which the drama was developing in several directions simultaneously. The need to justify a special study of the interludes is the fault of the historians of drama. When I began the research on which this study is based, I found a general prejudice against plays where allegory is employed for purposes of moral instruction. At worst, the moral interludes meet with frank hostility (". . . aridity and mortal dullness . . . merely transitional and abortive products . . .")[1]; at best, they are tolerated as a bridge between the miracle cycles and the admired morality *Everyman* on the one hand and the "Shakespearian" drama on the other, being allowed some historical significance but next to no dramatic merit.

It is my purpose to show that they were far more effective when acted than we can guess when we merely read them. The point here is not simply that a good performance may redeem a mediocre play—though music and spectacle must be taken into account, especially in interludes performed at court—but that so much of the meaning of many interludes is conveyed by the significant use of action and costume that unless this is borne in mind they cannot be appreciated or even properly understood. The dramatic conventions of the plays require more detailed consideration than they have yet received, partly for this reason and partly because no plays—those of the "Shakespearian" period not excepted—more thoroughly exploit their theatrical setting. Not all the interludes need an elaborate decorated background (though a few, court, plays do in fact profit from such a background); but they do all require an audience very close to the acting space, an audience which can be drawn into the play it is witnessing. An atmosphere of informality, far from casually resulting from an elementary form of drama, has in fact been carefully fostered by the dramatists. Even critics well disposed towards the Tudor interludes have not brought this point out adequately. The joint editors of *Fulgens and Lucrece*,[2] a play in which characters join the play from the audience to which they pretend to belong, comment:

> The consequence of this intermingling of actors and spectators is an imperfect sense of dramatic objectivity. On a number of occasions [references follow] the audience is addressed or referred to as if it were itself on the stage. But it would be a mistake to infer from the *naïveté* of Medwall's attitude in this matter of theatrical illusion, or from the primitive character of his "stage," that his dramatic technique is necessarily at all points crude . . .

and they proceed to praise his dramatization of his source, and such felicities as making one servant narrate to another the outcome of the play's central disputation between Lucrece's two suitors. These things are indeed merits; but the great dramatic achievement of the play arises wholly from the "imperfect sense of dramatic objectivity" which the editors find it necessary to excuse. Medwall, planning his interlude for performance in a banqueting-hall, without scenery, during the intervals of a banquet (to which there are several references) has recognized that it is impossible to insist that the dining spectators have been magically transported to ancient and romantic Rome. They are sitting at Cardinal Morton's familiar tables, as they well know; "Thay haue not fully dyned," and they continue their meal in the interval. This is a situation wholly different from that arising when spectators have paid to enter a building for the special purpose of being transported to an imagined place. Medwall's spectators are too conscious of their own business to be transported in this way: Rome must be served up to them; and in the process it must be made Tudor, not only because the contemporary setting enforces this contemporary treatment of incident and character, but also because the interlude has a contemporary moral theme (the true gentleman is known by his manners and not by his birth, being virtuous and not extravagant in dress or behaviour). Accordingly, in spite of a prologue which sets the play's action in the past, what the spectators witness is deliberately designed to appear to happen in present time and place. At the same time, everybody knows that it is a play (and based on an old story at that), and the dramatist exploits this knowledge. When, near the beginning, the servant called B decides to reply to Cornelius's request for a page, his companion A (they never get, and do not need, any better names) begs him not to do so:

> Be god thou wyll distroy all the play.

To which B retorts

> Distroy the play, quod a? nay, nay,
> The play began neuer till now.
> I wyll be doyng, I make god auow . . .

—both speaking verse, for all the colloquial urgency of their talk, and both evidently actors, even though both are standing among the spectators and B has emphatically denied (again in verse) that he is a player. Roper's famous story of Sir Thomas More, during his youthful service in this very household of Morton's, stepping suddenly in among the actors and making a part of his own extemporally there amongst them, though it may be apocryphal, admirably reflects the nature of theatrical illusion as cultivated by Medwall and his contemporaries and successors.[3] It was a dramatic form which was constantly pretending to burst its artistic limits, skilfully affecting to be on the verge of extemporization. There is a connexion here with those plays of Elizabeth's court (*Liberality and Prodigality*, Peele's *The Arraignment of Paris*) in which the dramatic action finally melts into courtly compliment as the actors suddenly come down before the Queen and address her. It is a dramatic tradition cultivated throughout Tudor drama.

This apparently precarious balance between the world of the play and the world of fact is also perceived in the use of boy actors by such dramatists as wrote for the boys' companies. In comedy, the piquancy of boys' playing feminine and adult characters is deliberately brought out for the spectators' amusement.

It is clear, then, that all these aspects of the interludes must be considered if we are to appreciate their merits and the skill of their authors. Such consideration has never, as far as I can discover, been given them. Though the settings required by the plays have from time to time been discussed (conspicuously by Sir Edmund Chambers) these settings have always been secondary in interest to the late Elizabethan public stage for which Shakespeare wrote. Undoubtedly many interludes have been ignored because they are capable of performance in a variety of settings. It remains to show what flexibility of dramatic construction this encouraged. The conventions of action and of dress have barely been touched on (though Dr M. C. Bradbrook has written valuably on the conventions of later Elizabethan and Jacobean drama); and here again detailed investigation is necessary.

In the first two chapters which follow, I hope to build up, by particular instances, some picture of the various settings in which the interludes were performed, and of the various actors (their numbers, their ages, their special talents) who most probably performed them. The two chapters following these will be concerned with the significant use of dress, its power of representing recognizable characters and its importance to the moral themes of the plays, with especial reference to changes of costume. In the last chapter I shall discuss some conventions of action and stage business, and shall finally try to reconstruct the dramatic effect of two representative interludes. The whole book is an attempt to show how the interludes impressed, and were meant to impress, their audiences.

The conclusions I have reached are based almost wholly on the internal evidence (that which the plays themselves provide).

The body of indisputable recorded fact about the performance of Tudor plays is well known to be small, and I have used only such source-material of this kind as has already been published. Much cannot be known with certainty (on the evidence clearly extant). My purpose has been to show what can reasonably be guessed or deduced; and I hope that it will be quite clear where facts end and conjecture begins, and that I have not too often allowed myself to be led into false emphasis and mistaken guesses by the evidence as it has seemed to me.

I began this study eight years ago as a piece of research later submitted for the degree of Ph.D. at Cambridge University. In my dissertation I discussed also the subjects and the moral intentions of the interludes. To limit this book to moderate length, and also to concentrate attention where it is most needed, I have here confined myself to reconsidering and expanding my original account of the performance of these plays.

It is pleasant to record many favours and generous acts with which I have met. Without the award of a Bachelor Scholarship, and subsequently of the Adelaide Stoll Bachelor Research Studentship, by the Master and Fellows of Christ's College, I could not have undertaken research. I have also received welcome grants from the Research Maintenance Grants Committee at Cambridge, and from the Research Board of Leicester University; to the Leicester University Press I am indebted for the publishing of this book. The staffs of the University Libraries of Cambridge and Leicester, and of the Bodleian and British Museum libraries, have given me great help, and I must not omit the excellent County Borough Library of Warrington. The illustrations, from the Bodleian and British Museum libraries, appear by their librarians' permission and have been reproduced by their photographic services. For help with the illustrations I am grateful to Mr A. E. Popham and Mr Edward Croft Murray of the British Museum, and to Mr E. C. Chamberlain of the Fitzwilliam Museum, Cambridge.

What I owe to members of the English Faculty at Cambridge is too large to be fully acknowledged here. My chief gratitude is due to Dr M. C. Bradbrook, Dr F. R. Leavis and Miss Enid Welsford. Miss Welsford supervised my research when I began to study the Tudor drama, and her support has been invaluable at all times.

During the preparation of this book for the press, I have enjoyed the benefit of Professor A. R. Humphreys's advice; and my dear wife also has given me every encouragement and much help.

T. W. C.

The University,
Leicester,
October 1957.

CHAPTER I

THE SETTING

In the introductory chapter I suggested that many critics who disparage the Tudor interludes do so because they have ignored the effectiveness of these plays in performance. I shall now discuss the stage requirements of the interludes, and hope to show how the dramatists exploited the conditions under which they expected their actors to work.

The history of the stage before 1600, though there will always be modifications of its details, is in general too well known to require a detailed re-statement. The works of Sir Edmund Chambers remain, and deservedly, the standard chronicles of this history.[1] It is necessary only to mention the principal forms of "stage" which were in use during the Tudor period.

The miracle plays were performed, according to the circumstances most appropriate, either on mobile "pageants" travelling through the town and halting at fixed stations, or in a single play-field surrounded by the separate stages of groups of characters. A detailed account of the mobile pageants as they appeared at Chester in the sixteenth century shows that they were two-storey vehicles, the lower storey serving as dressing-room and the upper as stage.[2] The action of each play in the cycle was confined to its own pageant, though at Coventry Herod "ragis in the pagond and in the strete also," which shows that the actors could either climb or leap down among the spectators if the occasion warranted it.[3] The other kind of performance is designed for a large open space (called in Latin *platea*, and in English "the place") in which most of the acting is done, though there is constant visible coming-and-going between "the place" and the separate scaffolds (or *sedes*) of the principal actors. The cycle known as the *Ludus Coventriae* or as the N-Town Plays requires this kind of setting. The scaffolds seem to have had curtains behind which the players retired when they were not engaged (for when a character re-enters the action he "sheweth him-self in his skafhald"), and behind which they might assemble in order to be revealed in an impressive tableau (the Convocation of the Jews, preparing to condemn Jesus, is so revealed in the same cycle when the council-house "xal sodeynly onclose").[4] The spectators are evidently grouped near to the "place," in such a way that they can see into all the separate scaffolds when the action requires it, but do not impede the actors who move to and fro.

There should now be mentioned an elementary form of stage which is not known to have been used for miracle plays, but which is well authenticated by the elder Pieter Bruegel and other sixteenth-century artists. This is simply a platform raised upon trestles, the front portion exposed to view and serving as stage, the back portion curtained off and serving as dressing-room. It appears frequently in pictures of actors performing in the street and at village fêtes.[5]

In contrast with the extreme simplicity of this trestle-stage backed by a plain curtain, settings were developed in the sixteenth century which were decorative and spectacular in intention, and which show a steady progress towards the realistic representation of place. At first there was devised (in the later fifteenth century) an arcaded stage, suitable to the performance of the classical Latin comedies which were being enthusiastically revived. Along the back of the acting-space there ran a series of curtained arches, each often labelled with the name of the character whose house it signified. Behind the barrier formed by these arches there was another space which accommodated actors who were resting between appearances, changing their dress, and so forth.[6]

This arcaded stage, though it might be elaborately decorated, was not representational so much as suggestive. It could, in fact, be described as the trestle-stage principle adapted, creating more entrances than the two round the edges of a curtain, and imaginatively identifying particular entrances with the houses of the characters who used them. These entrances acquired the name of "houses" from their function, and the history of English court drama in the sixteenth century is very largely the history of how these "houses" developed from a labelled door to a representational and three-dimensional structure of lath and painted canvas. Yet these realistic "houses" preserved the basic feature of the arcade-stage and even of the trestle-stage: they were joined together to form a false wall, corresponding to the trestle-stage's curtain, at the back of the acting-space; and behind this wall the actors could move about, unseen by the spectators. There were, of course, openings in this false wall besides the representational doors of the representational buildings, and one of the difficulties of court staging is that "house" or *domus* becomes the technical term for any part of that lath-and-canvas wall, whether it represents a building or (say) a forest.

At the end of the fifteenth century and the beginning of the sixteenth, however, these refinements of the setting do not seem to have been known; instead the actors performed in the banqueting-hall of their regular employer or their temporary host and simply used the setting which they found at their backs. Most Tudor halls follow a standard pattern, a pattern still to be seen in the halls of Oxford and Cambridge colleges. There are commonly two doors (sometimes three) in the wall nearest the kitchen, when a passage divides the kitchen from the hall; or at other times, particularly when the hall directly adjoins the kitchen, these two doors are in a wooden partition near the kitchen end of the hall. In either case these doors are called the screen doors, and the wall or partition in which they are placed is called the screen. In some halls, but not all, the screen supports a gallery.[7]

Indoor performance was, I think, the kind of performance for which most Tudor interludes were designed. Some plays are known to have been acted in a *platea*-and-*sedes* setting like that described for the *Ludus Coventriae* and used also in *The Castle of Perseverance*: two lost Protestant plays by James Wedderburn were acted, before 1540, at Dundee, one on the playfield and the other at the West Port of the town.[8] Bale's anti-Catholic trilogy of *God's Promises*, *John the Baptist*, and *The Temptation of Our Lord* was aggressively revived by the author at the market cross of Kilkenny on Mary's coronation-day; but the probable association of Bale with Cromwell's players in the 1530s makes it likely that he wrote his plays for indoor performance by that company rather than for acting out of doors. They can be acted in a variety of settings, his design evidently being to reach as wide a public as possible; and the Kilkenny performance may have been on a trestle-stage.[9] On the other hand, Lyndsay's expanded version (the only surviving version) of *Ane Satyre of the Thrie*

Estaitis, which was acted on the playfield at Edinburgh, is planned for that setting, and there is a pavilion for the actors' general use, as well as separate scaffolds for most of the important characters, not to mention a stream which plays an important part in the action.[10] But apart from adaptations (like Bale's) and elaborate public spectacles (Lyndsay's), Tudor interludes take place indoors. Chambers shows that several of them contain allusions to "this hall," and that most of them require no scenery, being content with an undefined acting "place" (the *platea*, perhaps, of the outdoor settings) and a door which can be used in the action. From this he concludes very naturally that, apart from specially decorative performances at court,

> the hall contemplated was at first just the ordinary everyday hall, after dinner or supper, with the sovereigns or lords still on the dais, the tables and benches below pushed aside, and a free space left for the performers on the floor, with the screen and its convenient doors as a background and the hearth ready to hand if it was wanted to figure in the action.[11]

This is thoroughly convincing, and may be accepted as the principle behind the staging of Tudor interludes in general. It remains to consider what variations on this type of setting are to be found (most of them are discussed by Chambers, whose evidence I wish to weigh afresh in some instances), and what profit the dramatists obtain from the kind of staging that they adopt.

There is little evidence that raised platforms were set up in halls for interludes before the second half of the sixteenth century.[12] Perhaps the first that calls unequivocally for a raised stage is *The Cobbler's Prophecy* (printed 1594), which Chambers has convincingly argued to be a court play (its plot and language, both strongly complimentary to the Virgin Queen, reinforce his views); its opening direction is:

> Enter *Iupiter* and *Iuno*, *Mars* and *Venus*, *Apollo*, after him, *Bacchus*, *Vulcan* limping, and after all *Diana* wringing her hands: they passe by, while on the stage *Mercurie* from one end *Ceres* from another meete.[13]

There is the hint of a raised stage in *All for Money* (printed 1578, perhaps written earlier), because of an early episode in which three characters vomit up their new-born sons; but the directions are (I think deliberately) ambiguous, and a raised "state," in which the fathers might sit, and between the legs of which the sons might crawl forth in turn from behind improvised hangings at its back, would meet the author's demands.[14] In *Apius and Virginia* (printed 1575, entered 1567–68), during an anguished soliloquy, "Here let *Virginius* go about the scaffold." A London citizen, Henry Machyn, writes in his diary of the setting up of "skaffolds" inside halls for plays in 1560 and 1562; and a "stage and Raile" was constructed at Trinity College, Cambridge, for John Foxe's *Christus Triumphans* in 1563.[15] Some of these scaffolds and stages (the terms are often synonymous in the sixteenth century) may just possibly have been for the accommodation of spectators and not actors. If they were for the actors, one has to choose between a platform low enough not to impede the doors of the screens or of the "houses" (probable in *The Cobbler's Prophecy* and *Apius and Virginia*, for both these plays seem to require some scenery) and a high trestle-stage with a curtained rear (perhaps *All for Money*, where no scenes are localized, even imaginatively).[16]

As for the use of a background of "houses," I think that there was less of it than Chambers is prepared to assume, and that it is confined mainly to Elizabethan court interludes of a professedly spectacular nature.

This question of "houses" may be first studied in plays where scenes take place in two different stated localities. In Lewis Wager's *Mary Magdalene* the action begins at Magdalo, whence Mary and the vice set off for Jerusalem, and it is at Jerusalem that the later episodes take place, the only localized one being at the house of Simon the Pharisee. Chambers, who believes that Simon's house was "some kind of open *loggia* with a table in it," conjectures that both Magdalo and Jerusalem were "indicated on opposite sides of the hall or stage, and that the personages travelled from one to the other over the intervening space, which was regarded as representing a considerable distance."[17] Though there was this kind of direct transfer from one represented locality to another in the *Ludus Coventriae* and in other plays outdoor and indoor (in, for instance, John Phillip's *Patient Grissell*),[18] I think a quite different way of signifying a journey was employed in *Mary Magdalene*. It is important that when the action at Jerusalem begins it is not Mary and the vice who speak, but Simon and Malicious Judgment, who are plotting to test Christ at a banquet. Soon the vice joins and assists them, boasting how he has corrupted

Mary, who must be out of hearing at this point. I think she is in fact off-stage, and reappears only when she begins to speak at Jerusalem, seventy-two lines after the vice's speech there begins. It would be impossible for Mary and the vice to represent their shared day's journey by crossing a hall's narrow breadth when there is so much time between their several arrivals at Jerusalem.[19] It is most probable, therefore, that they left at one entrance of the stage or hall, Simon and Malicious Judgment entering immediately at the other, to be shortly followed by the vice, and after some delay, by Mary. If this is so, there is no need of any visible indication of either Jerusalem or Magdalo, for the characters' speeches make it clear where they are supposed to be. Even Simon's house need not be a *domus*. There are signs that the table and stools, as well as the banquet, have to be brought out, and that both this and their removal take time.[20] Simon, so to say, brings in his house by virtue of his presence, and when he departs it ceases to exist. This interpretation of the staging is supported by the probability that the actors of *Mary Magdalene* were a travelling company and accordingly could not look for constructed scenery (see below, p. 30).

A basically similar situation is presented in Ingelend's *The Disobedient Child*. Here Chambers notes that "some episodes are before the house of the father, and others before that of the son in another locality forty miles away" and concludes that both localities were indicated.[21] But though it is possible to imagine this play acted in front of "houses," it is equally possible (and, I think, preferable) to imagine a performance dispensing with this scenic luxury. The fact that, after his quarrel with his father, the son departs with a cry of "room" implies that some spectators are standing around the screen-door through which he makes his exit (this practice will be discussed later). One of these screen-doors could represent the father's house in London throughout the play, while the other could be used mainly by characters at a distance (though not exclusively by them, for it also serves for the son's exit here, and is employed also in the final scene). Like Simon's house in *Mary Magdalene*, the son's house is the scene merely of a single episode near the end of the play, which would hardly repay the trouble of constructing a *domus*, especially as it is not clear from the text whether the action is within or without.[22] Other scenes at a distance from London take place at or near an inn where the son lodges before his marriage and where the (reported) wedding feast is held. All these scenes away from London could be acted with the characters using the door which was not the father's. But this other door never acquires any particular associations, a fact which is seen to be necessary at the end, when it is used by both son and father when approaching the father's house from the outside. First, "in commeth the Rychmans Sonne alone," uttering a rueful monologue as he nears his father's house. Immediately after this, "Here the Ryche man must be as it were commynge in." The careful phrasing makes it clear that he does not merely "come in" (to the "place") but that in so doing he creates the effect of "coming in" (to his house), and the indication that he proceeds like his son from the one door towards the other is confirmed by his final remark, "But yet come on, to my house wee wyll be goynge." In both these plays it would, I think, create an embarrassing distraction to represent buildings unless they were used or referred to throughout the action (as are the buildings in Lyly's plays or in the more spectacular of the court interludes).[23]

With these supposed "houses," and others which I consider equally illusory,[24] may be contrasted the specified "houses" in *Thersites* (probably an Oxford University play and written in 1537): Mulciber has "a shop made in the place," and Thersites' Mother has "the place which is prepareth [*sic*] for her." It is to be noted that both these are prescribed in the text; also, that both are put to active service (the former contains Mulciber's stock of armour wherewith he equips Thersites; the latter provides a hiding-place for that cowardly hero).

Whether the single buildings mentioned throughout *Jack Juggler* (Bongrace's house) and *Roister Doister* (Custance's house) were structural "houses" or mere doors is open to conjecture. Since both plays are neo-classical and have no changes of locality, their authors and producers may well have known something of the new fashion in staging (I call it new because it had been introduced only recently into English indoor performances). The siege of Custance's house in *Roister Doister*, during which Merrygreek fires an arquebus at it, certainly makes its representation desirable. I once thought that a structure might be built round one screen-door, leaving the other free for use by persons not dwelling in Custance's house (an extension of *The Disobedient*

Child's requirements); but I now believe that with very little extra trouble a whole lath-and-canvas street scene, of which a practicable *domus* formed the main part, could be constructed. This would undoubtedly be the best solution to the staging of *Gammer Gurton's Needle*, where *two* cottages are wanted, and Dame Chat's has a hole through which the unsuspecting Doctor Rat is enticed by Diccon to creep in order to practise amateur crime-detection. Indeed, the play could not be performed without a formal background of these *domus* unless there were three doors, two doing duty as the cottages and the third serving for independent entrances and exits. Even then, Dame Chat's would require carpenter's work around it to provide the hole for Rat; and so although there was in the sixteenth century a side-door in the hall of Christ's College, Cambridge (where the play was played, at least according to its title-page, "on Stage"), I now suppose that the original setting was a lath-and-canvas structure showing a street and two houses.[25]

The only "houses" that we can confidently assume to have been constructed for these plays are those which have a positive theatrical function (these, for instance, in *Thersites* and *Gammer Gurton's Needle*). It would have been possible, of course, to create a setting of "houses" when a particularly decorative performance of any interlude was intended, either at court or in a private house or in a college hall. As early as 1515, in a court disguising, there "sodainly came oute of a place lyke a wood .viij. wyldemen"; this description seems to imply a construction painted to look like a wood, rather than a collection of real or artificial trees.[26]

It is to the court and the colleges (including also the great houses and the Inns of Court) that we look for decorative and representational scenery, both because more records of performance at these places survive than of performance elsewhere, and because court and college revenues could best support the expense involved.[27] During the sixteenth century, it became particularly fashionable to construct a large, decorative, and eminently practical central "house," sometimes of two storeys, which dominated the setting. G. R. Kernodle has shown how this centre-piece developed from medieval art and pageantry and was in course of time to influence the elaborate façade of the Elizabethan public theatre's tiring-house. Both Chambers and Kernodle have analysed the action of *Horestes*, which they very reasonably identify with the *Orestes* listed in the court revels accounts for 1567–68:

The main structure is a castle gate with a battlemented gallery above and serves to symbolize several different cities in succession. Clytemnestra speaks from the walls above; the city is assaulted by an army; Aegisthus is hung from the battlements by means of a ladder; the army of Orestes makes a triumphant entry through the city gates; and then, as a final scene, Orestes is crowned king by Truth and Duty.[28]

Analysis of *The Marriage of Wit and Science* will show that a similar decorative and functional castle was its principal piece of scenery, and supports the frequent assumption that this interlude is the court *Wit and Will* listed in the same year as the court *Orestes*.[29]

At the beginning of the play Wit points out his beloved's house, and vows "Before I slepe I will to yonder forte repaire." At the opening of the second act he gives Will a message for Science. After a short monologue on his master, during which time he has seemingly been walking about the "place," Will announces "But now am I come to the gate of this Ladye," and stands aside "amonge these fellowes" to eye her as she enters ("these fellowes" are the adjoining spectators). She agrees to receive Wit "within this house of myne," and Will departs for "home." This ends the second act. At the beginning of the third, Will reappears with Wit, and before long they reach Science's house, where Wit is interviewed by her parents Reason and Experience, and is presented with the services of Instruction, Study, and Diligence.[30] All these now leave Science's parents at the house and depart off-stage (end of Act Three), to reappear in hot argument as to whether they shall return to get a sight of Science herself (beginning of Act Four). Once again they proceed to the house, meet Science, and learn from her of Tediousness, a giant who "lurketh in the woode, hearby." The description of his fierceness moves Study and Instruction to "retourn from whens we came" (that is, into Science's house), while Wit decides on instant battle and moves straight on to the "deadly denne," from which Tediousness emerges and strikes him down.[31] After passing through the hands of Recreation (who revives him) and of Idleness (who dresses him like a fool), Wit says "To Science now wyll I," and immediately he is speaking to her and Reason, evidently at her house once more. Assisted by a flogging from Shame, he soon repents his dalliance with Idleness and is invited to "Come in and dwell with vs" (all, except perhaps Shame, enter the house). An amusing episode follows when Will returns; he had been sent "home"—to Wit's home, that is—when Wit was dancing with Idleness, and he now seeks in vain for his master ("I left hym snorting here"). But as he stands bewildered in the "place,"[32] Wit reappears with Science, who promises to watch the second fight from "this Closet" (perhaps an upper window of the house). Aided by Instruction, Study, Diligence, and the eager Will, Wit again challenges and this time slays his foe, afterwards ordering "Now home a pace, and ringe it out, that Tediousnes is slayne." Science cries "I heare and see the ioyfull newes," runs out to welcome them, and takes them to inform her parents: "Come after mee all fiue, and I will lead you in." This majestic conclusion, with Wit bidding the audience a courteous farewell, as he and Science triumphantly enter the house, recalls the "Enter now we wyll the citie gate" of *Horestes*. Doubtless the castle stood centrally at the rear of the acting-space, flanked by the entrances used by Wit and Tediousness (both of which may have been representational *domus*) and another entrance used by Recreation, Idleness, and their respective attendants.

Liberality and Prodigality, another court play (perhaps—though this is not so certain—the *Prodigality* of 1567–68, the year of *Horestes* and *The Marriage of Wit and Science*), is exacting in its demands.[33] Again the principal structure is a palace (this time Fortune's), and most of the action takes place in or near it, though there are also incidents at two inns and (finally) in a court of justice where Prodigality is convicted of the murder of Tenacity. The palace is an elaborate construction (even the sordid miser Tenacity is moved to cry "Ah goodly Lord, how gay it is!"). It has an upper storey with a "stately sumptuous throne," wherein Fortune is ceremonially installed and whence she must "Come downe" before leaving the stage in her chariot. Through a window in this palace Prodigality tries to climb with the help of a ladder, but "Fortune claps a halter about his neck, he breaketh the halter & falles." Adjacent to Fortune's palace, and in vivid contrast to it, is Virtue's "homely bowre" (not otherwise described) in which she sits and presumably observes the action.

One of the inns has perhaps an upper storey, as the host speaks from his bedroom. The other inn, which is "hard by," need not be represented, though the fact that the hostess is personally abusing an off-stage cook when she appears makes it desirable. As for the court of justice, this is not wanted till the final scene, when (after the judge's formal entry) a direction "The Iudge placed, and the Clerkes vnder him" leaves open the possibility that the benches required were brought out specially into the "place." The "place" would then become the court-room, from which Prodigality's appeal to the Queen's mercy, and the final general obeisance, could be easily and directly made. The last direction, "Vertue, Equitie, Liberalitie, Iudge, and all come downe before the Queene, and after reuerence made, Vertue speaketh," suggests that the acting area may have been slightly raised, unless "downe" here means down the hall.[34]

Certain plays involve the use of a wood in some scenes and not in others. Here, as in the disguising of 1515 already mentioned, a "house" painted to look like a clump of trees seems to be wanted, especially as characters about to act scenes in the wood enter "out of the wood"; though in *Common Conditions*, from which this direction is taken, there is at least one solid tree to which a princess is tied by some robbers and up which the comedian climbs to outwit them. In *The Cobbler's Prophecy* there is a wood in which a duke goes hunting.[35] The action of Thomas Garter's *Susanna* is intelligible only if we imagine an acting area bisected by a partition which runs from the front to the back. This is the orchard wall. On the one side of it the orchard trees are represented, perhaps merely by a painted canvas; there is no need for an opening, for the play insists that there is only one way into the orchard, and that is a door in the wall. The detailed stage-directions make the action easy to follow. When the Elders have laid their plans, "they go afore into the Orchard, and Susanna and her two maydes come vpon the stage." After a few lines they also "goe into the Orcharde"; but now it proves that the maids have forgotten soap and oil for the bath, and so "Here they go out and shut the Orchard doore," leaving Susanna and the lurking Elders visible inside. It is a real door, for one of the maids bids the other, "Proue with your foote, if that the Dore, as we were bad be lockt"; and, this done, the action continues within the orchard: "Here they go out, and the two Iudges that lye hidden talke in this wise," attempting to seduce Susanna and pointing triumphantly to the fact that "the Orchard dores are fast, the walles are close and iust." Repulsed, they call out for witnesses to whom they may accuse her falsely. "Here two seruauntes of the house run out, and breake open the Orchard dore." Though one side of the stage (not, perhaps, so much as half) is evidently reserved to depict the orchard, the other side serves a variety of purposes, and accommodates (perhaps only temporarily) "a Table" where the Elders sit "turning of bokes," a judgment-seat for their trial, and a "stake" where they are stoned in bloodthirsty fashion. The chief importance of this play's staging is the formal division of the "place" by means of a wall, presumably of lath-and-canvas. Such a wall was ideally required for the artisans' play in *A Midsummer Night's Dream*:

QUIN.: Then there is another thing, we must haue a wall in the great Chamber; for *Piramus* and *Thisby* (saies the story) did talke through the chinke of a wall.

SN.: You can neuer bring in a wall. What say you *Bottome*?

BOT.: Some man or other must present wall . . .

The comedy of this extract depends, not upon the supposedly primitive expedients of our early drama, but upon the artisans' fantastic circumvention of what they ought to have been able to do; and the irony is the greater if it is Snug the joiner, the very man who should have built the stage wall, who sees the difficulty as insurmountable.[36]

At this point I may briefly summarize my argument. The staging of the Tudor interlude was basically utilitarian. There might be decorative and realistic "houses" built for performances where spectacle was thought desirable and within the means of the producer, but the authors seldom forgot that the plain banqueting-hall with its two doors was the setting in which the interlude had arisen and prospered. Even when the setting was fundamentally modified, as in *The Marriage of Wit and Science* and those other court plays with an elaborate functional centre-piece,[37] there was no wanton pursuit of decoration for its own sake, and settings and buildings which the action did not require to be frequently seen and used were not represented, even at court (instead, decoration was lavished on what was important). Adaptability is the most conspicuous feature of the staging, and the great majority of interludes could be performed anywhere.[38] It is to be remembered that nearly all the plays which I have been discussing so far, and a few that I have not discussed, are exceptional in that they bear the mark of having been designed for particular settings.

Yet even those plays in which scenic illusion is carried farthest have much in common with those requiring no scenery at all, such as *Hickscorner* and *Youth* and *The Four PP*. Like the performances of the miracle plays and of the plays of Shakespeare, the performances of the Tudor interludes are meant to draw the adjoining audience into the play. And spectators never so thoroughly adjoined the acting-space as in the Tudor hall, where the actors had, in Chambers's expressive phrase, to "rub shoulders all the time with the inferior members of their audience."[39]

This rubbing of shoulders was a literal matter. Characters frequently talk as though they must fight their way between the "place" and the screen-doors. When Merry Report has become Jupiter's crier in *The Weather*, he bustles about his business:

> Frendes a feloshyp let me go by ye
> Thynke ye I may stande thrustyng amonge you there?
> Nay by god I must thrust about other gere.

Such demands as this, usually expressed in a cry of "Room!", are very common, and they indicate that the plays where they occur made use of the real doors of the hall. It is not necessarily true, of course, that every character who cries for "room" is seriously hampered by the spectators' bodies. Very often the demand simply displays a self-important or quarrelsome disposition, and is to be compared with the disagreeable habit of thrusting others from the wall in the street. The opening words of the vainglorious coward in *Thersites*:

> Haue in a ruffler foorth of the greke lande
> Called Thersites, if ye wyll me knowe
> Abacke, geue me roume, in my way do ye not stand
> For if ye do, I wyll soone laye you lowe

may be compared with his later boast:

> Yes yes god wote, they geue me the wall
> Or elles with my clubbe, I make them to fall
> Backe knaues I saye to them, then for feare they quake
> And take me then to the tauerne and good chere me make.

And the dialogue accompanying Wrath's first entrance in *The longer thou livest the more Fool thou art* exposes such words as unnecessary bravado:

WRATH: Make roume, stande backe in the Deuils name
Stande backe or I will lay thee on the face.
INCONTINENCE: Marie stande thou backe with a verie shame,
Is there not roume inough in the place?
IDLENESSE: It is but a coppie of his countenaunce,
Wrath must declare his propertie.
INCONTINENCE: He is as whot as a vengeance,
Stande backe and geue him libertie.

It is equally significant that the virtuous characters never have occasion to ask for room. The habit is reserved for the comic and the disreputable. Nevertheless, though the bystanders were doubtless considerate and moved aside without prompting, there were enough of them to constitute an obstruction if the character was resolved to find one. At times it is necessary to clear a larger space in the hall for special incidents. Thus, in *Impatient Poverty*,

Here entreth the somner agayne, & pouerte foloweth him with a candell in his hande doyng penaunce aboute the place. And then sayth the somner.
SOM.: Rowme syrs auoydaunce
That thys man maye do hys pennaunce.

Most interludes seem to have been written for an audience of whom some are sitting and others standing. As early as the fifteenth-century play *Mankind* a social distinction appears to be drawn between the "sovereigns" who sit and the "brethren" who stand up. A collection is taken from this audience and there are hints that an inn is the place of performance, though whether indoors or in a courtyard it is not easy to decide; in any case there are frequent demands for "room."[40] Most of the early Tudor plays, of which the setting is usually a plain hall, seem to have had some standing spectators. In banqueting-halls, perhaps visitors and kitchen-servants made up the extra numbers; or, when the play did not accompany a meal—as it did in *Fulgens and Lucrece* or *Gentleness and Nobility*—most of the tables and benches may have been moved aside to create a large "place." There are bystanders at *Mundus et Infans*, to whose judgment Folly appeals when a touch is claimed against him during a match at bucklers. The bridled Inclination in *The Trial of Treasure* imitates a horse and bids the spectators near him "stande awaye" to avoid being kicked. Several such plays contain no sign that any spectators are seated, and these are normally the plays which require no scenery. Fulwell's *Like will to Like*, which is representative, has a vice (Nichol Newfangle) who twice speaks to people "standing by," and addresses a woman spectator who stands "in the Angle"; and when he is about to give the evildoers their reward he brings in "a Bagge, a Staffe, a Bottle, and two halters, going about the place shewing it to the audience" and singing "Trim marchandise trim trim" (evidently a street-cry) "as oft as he thinketh good." The phrase "in the Angle" (though it may merely be due to its rhyme with Newfangle) strongly implies the four walls of a hall; and there is the traditional "place" for acting, not a constructed stage.

Court and college plays seem to have had more seated spectators than plays elsewhere. Chambers notes that the audience of *The Cobbler's Prophecy* is invited to "sit and see" the action,[41] though we should remember that "sit and see" is also used in the first Chorus of Shakespeare's *Henry V*, a public theatre play. The phrase is, I think, recommended to authors by its alliteration, so that it is used even when it applies only to a part of the audience. In *Susanna*, which employs a constructed orchard wall and which probably belongs to the court, a remark is made about "those that stand by"; and there are at least some bystanders at *The Marriage of Wit and Science* and *Gammer Gurton's Needle*.[42]

Three interludes—*All for Money*, *The longer thou livest the more Fool thou art*, and *The Conflict of Conscience*—are of interest because members of their audiences are urged to remove their hats in token of respect towards certain characters, but I do not think that this suggests an outdoor performance of any of them. To wear a hat indoors was not so eccentric in the sixteenth century as it is today. Moreover, since the audience's overt homage is not likely to be paid to Sin or Fortune, and still less to a Cardinal in an anti-Catholic play, demands for such homage are merely proud gestures towards the spectators (as when, again in *All for Money*, the vice bids them all kneel to Money); and so there is no question of removing hats, and therefore no reason why these plays should not have been acted indoors before a hatless audience.

It is not generally easy to determine where the interludes were acted by means of identifying the spectators, for not many plays are unmistakably addressed to particular audiences; the usual mode of address, in prologues and epilogues, is the formal one of "worshipful audience," "all this presence," "seemly sirs," or "sovereigns."[43] The "good people" of *King Darius* (both prologue and epilogue) and the blunt "all you present" of *The longer thou livest the more Fool thou art* suggest a popular audience, while at the upper end of the social scale are the patrons directly addressed in certain plays or mentioned as witnessing them. The second part of *Nature*, we are told, is to take place "whan my lord shall so deuyse" (the author was Cardinal Morton's chaplain), and Little Dick in *The Weather* has heard that Jupiter has come down "this night to suppe here wyth my lord," who was probably Henry VIII. *Wealth and Health* and *Liberality and Prodigality* have epilogues addressed respectively to Mary and Elizabeth.[44] The closing prayer of Redford's *Wit and Science*, wishing

> To our most noble kyng & quene in especiall
> to ther honorable cowncell / & then to all the rest
> such Ioy as long may reioyse them all best,

suggests that perhaps this play too enjoyed royal patronage, "all the rest" being the other spectators.

At the end of *Jack Juggler*, the page Jenkin (who has been so unmercifully fooled by the hero that he has been unsure of his own name) says to the audience:

> And for you also maister[s] I thinke it best
> You go to bede, and take your rest . . .
> I praye god geue you all good nyght
> And send you better hape, and fortune
> Then to lesse [*i.e.*, lose] your selfe homward as I haue don.

This is a speech of dismissal (rendering superfluous the rhyme-royal epilogue which follows) which shows that at least some of the spectators, having witnessed an evening performance, are leaving to go home.[45]

Besides prologues and epilogues (which are sometimes formal and sometimes, as here in *Jack Juggler*, informal) there are continual addresses to the audience in the action itself, as is to be expected when some of the spectators are very close to the actors. I shall shortly illustrate how effective was this direct addressing of the audience. At present I am concerned with the tone of the remarks. These should not be taken too literally as showing the audience's social quality and hence the place of performance. It must be remembered that it is usually the comic and disreputable characters (those who call for "room") who utter these personal remarks; also, that they speak mainly to bystanders adjoining the "place"—the least dignified members of the audience.

Sometimes a courteous apology for the lack of due respect suggests a courtly audience. Thus Heywood's *Love* begins with the arresting dramatic novelty of a young man walking about in moody silence. He is the melancholy Lover-Not-Loved, and his first words are an excuse for his disregard of the audience's "stately porte," leading naturally to a complaint of his unrequited passion. Another episode implying dignified spectators occurs in *Calisto and Melibea*, where the young lover Calisto departs with a respectful "Thus farewell my lordes" and immediately the bawd Celestina bustles in with the irreverent and colloquial

> Now the blessyng that our lady gaue her sone
> That same blessyng I giue now to you all
> That I com thus homely I pray you of pardon . . .

Much of the amusement in *Gentleness and Nobility*, where the rude Ploughman denounces aristocrats, refuses to grant to them more true gentility than to himself, and scorns to envy them, depends on the play's being performed before an aristocratic audience. An anachronistic passage of some twenty lines in *Susanna*, where the heroine's two maids complain amusingly that their illusions about the pleasures of court life are shattered—

> For we but wayters are on them, that leade these happy dayes,
> We trudge and trauayle and take payne, they do possesse the prayse—

is not about Palestine but about the courtly world to which the play has been brought as entertainment. At times, characters speak with extravagant and calculated rudeness about bystanders. The vice in *Like will to Like* shouts a question to "Jone with the long snout." In *Jack Juggler*, when the knavish hero has fooled the servant Jenkin, and Jenkin is asked by his master to smell out whether this villain is hiding among the spectators, Jenkin inspects them and replies:

> Trulye good syr by your maistershipps fauoure
> I cannot well fynd a knaue by the sauoure
> Many here smell strong but none so ranke as he.

The comedian of Heywood's *The Weather*, Merry Report, hears the hunting Gentleman wind his horn outside and affects to blame flatulent spectators for the noise; and when the Gentleman has come in, he praises him with the equivocal line "He would hunte a sow or twayne out of this sort" ("Here he poynteth to the woman."). The liberty of speech here suggests that the privileges of the outspoken court-fool were also enjoyed by the comedians of the interludes.[46]

It is now time to sum up the advantages which the interludes obtained from the principles on which they were staged. The main point to be made is that the close contact between the actors and the spectators, an inheritance from the established medieval methods of performance, was carried further in the Tudor halls. Though it might be supposed that the increasing sense of literary decorum and the development of scenery at court and elsewhere would push the play back away from the audience, this was not so. The background of "houses," when used, would admittedly cause the nearest spectators to group themselves in front of the acting space; whereas in the plays without scenery the spectators, if they stood on either side of both screen doors, might almost encircle the actors. But in all the plays alike, the characters continue to direct their quips and confidences at the audience and to mingle with it. Will, in *The Marriage of Wit and Science*, and Diccon, in *Gammer Gurton's Needle* (both plays with scenery), observe other characters from this vantage-point, and Pithias perhaps conceals himself there in order to intercept his friend Damon "by the way," as he is being led to execution.[47] Even if some of these plays employed a raised stage as well as scenery (which I do not think was often the case), it cannot have been a high one when characters slip so easily among the spectators. This was an advantage which neither the miracle play's pageant nor Shakespeare's theatre enjoyed.

In my introduction, I have suggested the importance of this relation between the players and the spectators, and I wish to return to it here. The reason for so much direct address is not that an audience so near the actors must be spoken to because it cannot be ignored. On the contrary, direct address is just one means whereby continual contact with the audience is sought and maintained. The spectators are encouraged to join in. Their excitement is whipped up by appeals like this of the depraved

Imagination in *Hickscorner* (his companion Freewill has just been converted by Contemplation and Perseverance, and has urged him to repent likewise):

> By goddes sydes I hadde leuer be hanged on hye
> Naye that wolde I not do I hadde leuer dye
> By goddes passyon and I hadde a longe knyfe
> I wolde bereue these two horesones of theyr lyfe
> How how twenty pounde for a dagger.

There is not a single Tudor interlude in which the audience is not brought in to the action in this way, and though it would be pleasant to give other instances they could only underline what is already clear. It is worth while, however, to stress the importance of the special excursions which are made, chiefly by the comic characters, among the spectators. Some of these would not be out of place at the modern circus and pantomime (perhaps, along with Punch and Judy, the last strongholds of genuine participation in a dramatic action by an audience). When the vice in Heywood's *Love* announces that the mistress of the Lover Loved has just been burned with her house (a report which only the Lover is meant to take seriously), he comes "ronnyng sodenly aboute the place among the audyens with a hye copyn tank [tall hat] on his hed full of squybs fyred," while spectators and squibs scatter in all directions. In *Wit and Science*, when Wit awakes from slumber and sees in his mirror that Idleness has blackened his face, he first suspects that something is wrong with the glass, and so he experiments among the audience:

> hah / goges sowle / what have we here a dyvyll
> this glas I se well hath bene kept evyll
> goges sowle a foole / a foole by the mas
> what a very vengeance aylth this glas
> other this glas is shamefully spotted
> or els am I to shamefully blotted
> nay by goges armes I am so no dowte
> how looke ther facis heere rownd abowte
> all fayre & cleere they evry chone
> & I by the mas a foole alone

The last couplet quoted is clearly a conclusion reached after a period of silent investigation; silent, that is, except for the laughter of the spectators as Wit's suspicion turns to certainty and leads to the expected lengthy wrathful outburst.

It is hard to resist the conclusion that sometimes a confederate might be planted in the audience. The prodigal hero of *The Disobedient Child* is reduced to selling faggots for his living:

> Ho thou good felowe which standest so nye
> Of these heauy bundelles ease my sore backe:
> And somewhat therfore gyue me by and by
> Or els I dye, for Syluer I do lacke.
> Now that I haue some Monye receyued
> For this my burden home I wyll go . . .

Money certainly seems to be handed over here, and the prodigal gets rid of his faggots and returns to where his wife awaits him. This is in the same dramatic tradition as the half-pretence that ordinary bystanders join the action in *Fulgens and Lucrece*: it was indeed not easy to "know a player from another man."[48]

In this chapter I have tried to show how the vigorous relationship between the actors and the spectators was encouraged by the settings in which the interludes were played. Everyone was in the play. Though there was a "place" reserved for the physical action, the dramatic action was limited only by the four walls of the hall.

CHAPTER II

THE PERFORMERS

VERY few facts are known about actual performances of Tudor interludes; and it has always been a matter of conjecture to assign particular plays to particular groups of actors, except on those rare occasions when documentary evidence about a performance survives. As I have implied in the previous chapter, even when the records of the court drama mention an *Orestes* or a *Wit and Will* or a *Prodigality*, it cannot be taken as certain that these plays are the *Horestes*, the *Marriage of Wit and Science*, and the *Liberality and Prodigality* that survive in printed texts, however probable the stage requirements of the extant plays may make this assumption. The same kind of doubt attaches to the companies performing the plays: it is usual for the court records to list the performing companies, but less usual (at least before 1580, by which time I take most of the plays I am discussing to have been written) to assign particular plays to them. This characteristic of the court records is (as will be expected) more pronounced still in the records of performances elsewhere. In general, when one is confronted with the printed text of a Tudor interlude, there is no indication of where or by whom it was acted, or indeed of whether it had received any performance. Normally, then, the plays themselves must be consulted if we wish to discover their probable settings and actors.

Sometimes the prologues make it clear that the performers were boys: the prologue to *Respublica*, drawing an intentionally comic contrast between "we children" and "youe olde folke" (Mary and her court) and justifying the handling of serious matters by "boyes," shows that it is written for child actors; and so are *Liberality and Prodigality* (where the prologue speaks of their "childish yeeres"), *Jack Juggler*, and *Tom Tyler*.

A distinction must first be drawn between these companies of boy actors and the adult companies. Sir Edmund Chambers and W. J. Lawrence have put forward most of what is known. The adult companies were the smaller groups, still averaging from four to six players in the first half of Elizabeth's reign, though their numbers gradually increased with the prosperity of the public theatres.[1] During the period of the Tudor interludes a professional adult company (even the royal company of Court Interluders) means a small company. The children's companies, of which the Children of the Chapel Royal and the boys of St Paul's choir school were the most important, were larger: the number of Chapel Children was fixed at twelve in 1526.[2] This difference in numbers may be assumed to have influenced the plays written for adult and for child companies. The adult actors would require either plays which introduced only a few characters (such as the majority of John Heywood's comic disputations) or plays where the characters were introduced either in sequence or in small alternating groups (as in Lupton's *All for Money* or in Fulwell's *Like will to Like*). The children, on the other hand, could present more characters at once, and were under little or no necessity of doubling the parts. This is not to say, of course, that they could not equally well perform those plays which I have just listed as suitable to adult companies: the plays of Heywood are particularly difficult to assign to their original actors, and his occasional association with the Paul's Boys during his career as a dramatist has suggested to Chambers that all his plays may have been written for them.[3]

It is also a matter of conjecture whether the masters of the children's companies continued to take part in their plays after the early years of the sixteenth century. There is recorded a play of *Troilus and Pandar*, given in 1516 by the Chapel Children, in which their master William Cornish played Calchas and a herald;[4] and Machyn's statement that Elizabeth was entertained at Nonsuch on 7 August 1559 with "a play of the chylderyn of Powlles and ther Master Se[bastian Westcott], Master Phelypes, and Master Haywood"[5] suggests that the adults may have taken some active part in the performance as well as organizing it. In the *Damon and Pithias* of Richard Edwards, the shaving of an adult "father Grim the collier" by two small mocking pages who were in real life his pupils would be a pleasant sight. However, we have to resist this kind of speculation. Probably the growing force of decorum as an artistic theory would discourage the appearance in the same play of adult actors and children acting adults (the play calls for a children's company and the pages are the only child characters in it). I shall also suggest later that this scene would have an equal, though different, comic force if played by three children.

There is also, besides the professional companies, the possibility of amateur acting in the Tudor period. Some plays, *Thersites* and *Gammer Gurton's Needle*, can be connected with the universities, and it is reasonable to suppose that they were acted by students.[6] Again, schoolmasters might encourage performances by their pupils, and Chambers suggests that some moral interludes may have been written and published specially for sale to such buyers.[7] That there were such groups seems very likely, but as scarcely anything is known of them I shall not attempt to guess their importance in the Tudor drama's development. It should be pointed out, however, that many published interludes, with their directions about the size of the company for which they are suitable, imply the existence of groups (either professional or amateur) with the will and the means to play them; they are not addressed to readers but rather to actors, and the technical merit of some of them suggests, to me at least, that their authors had some practical experience of writing for actors (I am here thinking particularly of William Wager's interludes).

In this chapter I shall not be attempting to prove the association of particular plays with particular companies, but to show, from the plays themselves, how certain plays are appropriate to certain kinds of company, and how the authors made use of the structure and the talents of the companies for which they wrote. I shall discuss first the distribution of a given number of rôles among a smaller number of actors (or doubling), then the action and characterization of the interludes, and lastly the use of vocal and instrumental music.

Many interludes carry on their title-pages such statements as "Eight persons may easely play this Commody" (Phillip's *Patient Grissell*). These statements are not always truthful, however, and the one just mentioned is an example of a false advertisement, presumably by the publisher, who wishes to sell the play to a company smaller than that for which the author has inconsiderately designed it.[8] Other examples are afforded by the anti-Protestant *Wealth and Health* and Lewis Wager's anti-Catholic *Mary Magdalene*, which are offered to companies of four actors but require five. The direct complimentary address to Mary at the end of *Wealth and Health* proves that this interlude was written for acting at court; it is probably the adult actors' equivalent of the children's *Respublica*.[9] The actors of *Mary Magdalene* are itinerant professionals, for the prologue contains the claim "We haue ridden and gone many sundry waies" and offers value for the audience's money "whether you geue halfpence or pence." Their statement "Yea we haue vsed this feate at the vniuersitie" may be taken either as literally true of this company or as referring generally to the practice of acting at universities. The title-page recommends the play as profitable to those who "heare or reade the same." Phillip's *Patient Grissell*, with its large cast and its songs for women characters, is clearly a play for children. It is highly probable that all these plays with faulty advertisements of doubling had been performed before they were printed and offered to unsuitable companies by their publishers.

It is easy to be too confident about the evidence supplied by the doubling of parts, and W. J. Lawrence seems over-optimistic when he writes:

> Armed with this knowledge [that five actors was the usual complement of a professional troupe in the early and much of the later sixteenth century], and given the number of actors in a play of specific, or approximately accurate, date, the student should have no difficulty in determining for what kind of actors and what kind of audience the play was written.[10]

This statement assumes that doubling was practised exclusively by the adult companies. There are, however, signs that the children's companies also dealt in this way with the minor parts. At the end of *Jacob and Esau*, a play with eleven characters, a song is performed by all the characters except Isaac's two neighbours Hanan and Zethar, who vanish after their single early scene and whose actors may now reasonably be supposed to be representing Isaac and "the Poete" (or epilogue-speaker). Another final ensemble is in Ingelend's *The Disobedient Child*, in which play there are ten characters. After the Perorator's moral summing-up comes the direction "Here the rest of the Players come in and kneele downe all togyther, eche of them sayinge one of these Verses," and there follow five quatrains containing the customary prayers for Elizabeth and for her clergy, nobility, and commons. Unless some actors came on here and said nothing, it looks as though the rôles were divided among the actor playing the

Perorator and five other actors. This could easily be done, as the play is from a Latin dialogue source, and never brings on more than three characters at once; some characters (the man and woman cooks, the priest, the servant, the devil) have only temporary parts in the action. Yet it seems like a boys' play (the hero is of school age when it begins), and is probably the "enterlude for boyes to handle and to passe tyme at christinmas" entered to its publisher Thomas Colwell in 1569–70;[11] while there can be no doubt at all that *Jacob and Esau*, with its boy-servants and the songs so prominent in its action, is also written for children.

While we must accordingly allow for the doubling of parts in children's as well as adults' plays, it is true to say that this practice is more characteristic of the adult companies. It is a practice to which both More and Erasmus refer as a thing well known, and which had been in use since at least the later fifteenth century.[12] Most of the earliest Tudor interludes are capable of arrangement for doubling, though they do not carry statements that this is so, and even long plays with large casts, like Medwall's *Nature* and Skelton's *Magnificence*, could be performed by half-a-dozen actors.[13] In Medwall's *Fulgens and Lucrece*, too, the absence of the heroine's father at the final scene suggests that the actor in question was now playing Flaminius, her successful suitor. All these early Tudor plays—*Youth*, *Hickscorner*, *Everyman*, *Calisto and Melibea*, *Nature*, *Magnificence*, *Gentleness and Nobility*, *The Four Elements* (an incomplete play), *Mundus et Infans*, and *Fulgens and Lucrece*—could be, and probably were, acted by adult professionals, if "adult" is legitimately extended to allow for one or two youths to take feminine rôles. The other early Tudor interludes of importance, John Heywood's plays, could also be acted either by adults or children, with the one exception of *The Weather*. In this play the ten characters appear together in the final scene, and a company of boys is consequently called for; the characters include two women (a Gentlewoman and a Laundress) and a boy ("the leste that can playe"—the direction implies that the other players are also boys, and that to act a real boy the smallest is wanted). And though the obscenities of Merry Report about his wife would come strangely from a boy actor, this may have been intended by Heywood as one of the absurdities of the piece, or (more likely) may spring simply from his delight in quibbles, punning, and fantastic innuendo.

John Bale, whose "fellows" performed before Thomas Cromwell late in 1538 and early in 1539, seems at that time to have enjoyed Cromwell's patronage and written for his professional adult company, though fourteen of his plays had already been dedicated to the Earl of Oxford, being perhaps acted by a company belonging to that nobleman.[14] Of his surviving plays, *Three Laws* and the trilogy *God's Promises*, *John the Baptist*, and *The Temptation of Our Lord* could all be performed by five actors. Lawrence denies that this is possible in *Three Laws*, but it can be done provided that there is a short break before the beginning of Act Five, during which Vindicta Dei can change for Deus Pater; as this break would not interrupt a piece of continuous action, but would merely isolate the *dénouement*, it seems allowable.[15] Bale's *King John* requires separate consideration, since it presents special difficulties. The manuscript in which it survives has been extensively revised in the author's own hand, and the latter part is written entirely in it. There are certain directions about the doubling of characters, but these are not always consistent with the action, even with that of the first part of the manuscript (not in Bale's hand) to which they are confined. Whether they represent Bale's own intentions at any time is not clear. These flaws in the doubling, together with modern commentators' persistent habit of treating as separate characters the temporary incarnations Stephen Langton, the Pope, Pandulphus, Raymundus, and Simon of Swynsett, have obscured the fact that there are not nineteen characters, to be acted by nine or even twelve players, but fourteen, who need be acted by only six (these fourteen include the Interpreter, whose expository speech, dividing the play into two acts, is Bale's later interpolation):

1. King John, Imperial Majesty.
2. England, Clergy, the Interpreter.
3. Sedition (= Stephen Langton).
4. Nobility, Private Wealth (= Pandulphus).
5. Civil Order, Dissimulation (= Raymundus, = Simon of Swynsett), Commonalty.
6. Usurped Power (= the Pope), Treason, Verity.

Lawrence's argument that "the twelve players who, in or about 1539, acted the nineteen characters in Bale's transitional morality of *Kynge Johan* were not professionals" accordingly fails.[16] The above distribution of the parts, furthermore, is based on the existing manuscript text completed in 1561, a revision and almost certainly an expansion of the original version, which may accordingly be believed to have been acted by Cromwell's professionals (assuming that company to have reached the standard number of six players), though each actor would have a heavier task than in Bale's earlier and less monumental plays.[17]

After the plays of Heywood and Bale, we may take those of an Elizabethan writer of moral interludes, William Wager. They are representative of the plays which Chambers suspects of having been published in the hope of thereby receiving a performance. All three of them (if we omit the fragment of *The Cruel Debtor* and assume, on good evidence,[18] that *The Trial of Treasure* is Wager's) contain statements of doubling; and in *Enough is as good as a Feast* two directions show that the doubling has been arranged by the author. Both these directions are addressed to the same actor. When, as Precipitation, he leaves the stage along with Worldly Man and Covetous (neither of whom is doubled with other characters), the direction "go out al .iii. togither and make you redy straight waies" bids him prepare for his coming entry as the downtrodden Tenant (the interval is filled by a choric speech of three rhyme-royal stanzas in which Heavenly Man reflects on Worldly Man's perilous spiritual state). Later, when he has been afflicting the Worldly Man in the character of God's Plague, he must "Go out and stand at the door" in order to enter some eighty lines later as the Physician. The fact that the four other actors who each play more than one part are not thus informed of their changes might suggest that the play was printed from this actor's copy, but this is most unlikely in view of other acting directions to the cast at large, notably to the vice Covetous, whose rôle involves much clownage. A curious feature is that, though Wager is clearly responsible for these instructions and for the consistent distribution of parts on the title-page, the action is held up for costume-changes at three points. When the reformed Worldly Man is cheerfully escorted from the stage by Heavenly Man and Contentation, the latter must return directly as Temerity and sing with his fellow-vices in praise of their leader Covetous. When Worldly Man has made a wretched and unrepentant end, Covetous and Ignorance depart in triumph, leaving the body alone on stage until carried off by Satan, who is the actor of

Ignorance in a different rôle; and at the end of his monologue Satan departs, to reappear as Contentation immediately afterwards. This is the more strange since a slight revision of the doubling would prevent these interruptions,[19] and since Wager's directions to another of the actors insist so urgently on continuous action. Only the second of these incidents, concentrating the audience's attention on the corpse of the sinner, gains any effectiveness from a pause in the action; the first, with the riotous entry of the vices forming a strong contrast with the sober departure of the virtues, would suffer by a delay. One concludes either that Wager was indifferent to pauses so long as they did not hold up an episode in the middle, or that he could not see how the doubling could be improved; or perhaps there was a quick-change artist in the company for which he wrote, since all these rôles are played by the same actor.

It is also curious that whereas this play calls for seven actors, *The Trial of Treasure* needs five and *The longer thou livest the more Fool thou art* only four. If Wager had a single company in mind it must have been a fluctuating one. It remains possible, of course, that a company's numbers could vary in this way. But I should not like to rule out the possibility that Wager wrote for children, even though he doubled his plays for small groups; *The longer thou livest the more Fool thou art*, with its abundant Latin quotations and the humour of beating the intractable young fool Moros at the beginning of the play, seems particularly apt to schoolboy performance.

An interlude undoubtedly designed for men is Thomas Lupton's *All for Money*. Though it differs from most other Elizabethan interludes in carrying no statement of doubling, its thirty-two characters could be easily shared among half-a-dozen energetic players. It employs the odd device of allowing an adult actor to make comic capital out of his maturity (the complementary process, a boy actor exploiting his boyhood, is more common and will be discussed later). Sin, the vice of the play, is brought physically to birth on the stage, being vomited up by his father Pleasure. The following dialogue ensues:

PLEASURE: Although my paynes were great yet nowe I may be glad,
That I haue to my sonne such a pretie fine ladde.
SINNE: If I be nowe a ladde, what be you than?
A boy of my age will neuer make man:

And although I be yong yet am I well growne,
No child of sixe yere olde is so bigge in all this towne.

Later, when he serves as court-usher to the corrupt judge All for Money, he is commanded to proclaim the sessions open, and asks

Shall I in my mannes voyce or in my boyes voyce it declare?
AL FOR MON.: So that it be heard I do not greatly care.

The vice is evidently an adult actor ("A boy of my age will neuer make man"), affecting a child's voice and causing amusement by allowing it to break from time to time into the deeper tones of a man. Lupton seems to have carefully avoided female characters. Only one appears, and she is a grotesque figure, a centenarian eager to buy a husband. An incident has also been adapted from one of Latimer's sermons, dealing with an infanticide who bribes the judge and is therefore released, whereas a petty thief is hanged because he is moneyless; in Latimer's sermon both these characters are women, but Lupton keeps the first off the stage (she sends a letter) and substitutes a man for the second, in spite of the extra moral force he could have given the scene by showing the judge's cruelty towards a woman.[20]

In contrast with these plays and others which employ doubling, and which are evidently designed for small companies, are those plays which can be acted only by a large company (of children), even though they may carry no explicit statement to this effect. Thus the siege of Custance's house in *Roister Doister* needs the participation of Merrygreek, Custance, Ralph, Tibet, Annot, Madge, Truepenny, Doughty, and Harpax, besides "Two drummes with their Ensignes," and before it is over Tristram Trusty also appears. The tendency to employ "extras" (seen here in the form of two drummers and two standard-bearers) is practically peculiar to the plays of the children's companies; but there seems to be an exception in *King Darius* (a rough-and-ready piece modelled on Bale's anti-Catholic plays and divided among six, probably adult, players) where four "extras" are wanted to play the king's guests and speak a few lines apiece. Other "extras" are the singing attendants of Fortune, and the kings drawing her chariot, in *Liberality and Prodigality*, the nine singing Muses in *Damon and Pithias*, twelve jurors to condemn the prodigal-turned-robber in *The Nice Wanton*, a "chappell" who sing a solemn hymn while the queen prays for the Jews in *Godly Queen*

Hester (there are also the "manye maydens" from whom the king selects his queen, and the many men attending on Haman), and two armies who fight a realistic battle in *Horestes* ("Go & make your liuely battel & let it be longe eare you can win the Citie"); *Horestes* is divided among six actors, but I suspect that this is the publisher's work rather than the author's, since the part of Idumeus is given to two of the actors though it does not need to be halved. The conspicuous use of "extras" in these plays, along with other features which I shall discuss shortly, strongly suggests the large resources of the boys' companies. The practice of doubling, on the other hand, suggests the adult companies, though it was not (as has been supposed) confined to them.

While the doubling of parts can tell us only a little about the structure of the acting company, it can tell us a good deal about the dramatist's art, and about the art of the actor.

I must insist at this point that there are more ways than one of constructing a play, and that the authors of interludes are often unjustly blamed for their deliberately chosen methods as though they were employing them by accident. It has, for instance, been suggested that the writers of Elizabethan interludes ran heedlessly after "profuse characterization":

> The wise morality writer was sensible enough to confine himself to a small cast of characters, a number little in excess of the number of his exponents; by this means he attained group acting and fuller play for the cut and thrust and parry of his dialogue. To this small band the authors of *Hickscorner* and *The Interlude of Youth* belonged. But the great majority disdained to cut their suit according to their cloth, and, heedless of the fact that unrestraint condemned them to a constructive system which meant a series of duologues, diversified only by an occasional soliloquy, aimed simply at profuse characterization.[21]

It is worth while to examine the construction of some Tudor interludes with this statement in mind. A play which implicitly demands the doubling of its characters, though it does not carry a statement of doubling, is *All for Money*, which I have recently mentioned. The central scene, from which the interlude takes its name, is the interviewing of six suitors by the corrupt judge All for Money. Before this court scene, there is first a complaint by Theology, Science, and Art, then the appearance of Money and his descendants Pleasure, Sin, and Damnation (each vomited up by his father), then a dispute between a virtuous rich scholar, a virtuous poor one, a rich and ignorant miser, and a cheerful beggar (all arguing wherein true happiness consists); and after the court scene, the despairing souls of Judas and Dives are driven over the stage by Damnation. It is true that most of these characters (with a few exceptions, like Sin the vice) do not return after a single appearance. It should be noted, however, that this structure is the result not of Lupton's capricious desire to present a wide range of characterization, but of his moral aim, which is to denounce greed by representing it in all the variety of its contemporary and general forms. Each of the incidents is related to the others and is partly interpreted by them (there are cross-references and reminiscences, such as the amusing interview between Sin and his grandfather Money just before the judge's session; and the final scene of damnation, though it is designed to shock the audience by immediately following the court scene, is the necessary end). To censure the play for "rambling diffuseness"[22] is to ignore its real structure, which is based on its moral thesis that the pleasures of materialism are damnable. Lupton attempts to show how society at large is greedy and ungodly, and the purpose of the long sequence of suitors is to give topical form to the general complaints of Theology, Science and Art, and also to the general boasts of Money and his descendants, earlier in the play, while the damned souls of Judas and Dives (the latter representing all cruel misers) bring the play back to its general moral subject.

It is quite certain that although the doubling of rôles encouraged the display of varied characters, this would have been attempted in any case. John Heywood's *The Weather* introduces a series of petitioners to Jupiter, each speaking for a trade or a social group, and all dissatisfied with the weather they receive. Though there are amusing clashes between the Wind-Miller and the Water-Miller and between the Gentlewoman and the Laundress, these petitioners are interviewed successively by Jupiter's servant Merry Report, and at the end of the play (there being no doubling) they assemble to hear Jupiter's decision to give them the weather as it was. Here again it is the subject, not the company's size, that has dictated the form of the play; and the social criticism of such Elizabethan interludes as *All for Money* could hardly have been expressed by any other method.

At the same time, while allowing that the author's moral design usually requires him to display a series of social type-figures, it might be argued that this, and the consequent need to double the parts, has made the construction somewhat mechanical. In Ulpian Fulwell's *Like will to Like*, vicious characters appear in pairs in order that the vice Nichol Newfangle may "join like to like alway"; and accordingly Newfangle interviews Rafe Roister and Tom Tosspot, Hance and Philip the drunken Flemings, and Cuthbert Cutpurse and Pierce Pickpurse. But in spite of this formal design, and of having only five actors at his disposal, Fulwell is not reduced to bringing in the characters without regard to natural probability and dramatic effect. On the contrary, he rises to the challenge of his subject, emphasizing that characters need not go out simply so that others may come in. After their scene with Newfangle, Tosspot and Roister are just going out when Nichol pulls them back:

> Cum again for you shal not so sodainly be gon.
> See you not who cums yonder an old frend of yours,
> One that is redy to quasse at all houres.[23]

With that, Hance comes in with a merry song, and it is not until his drunkenness has been fully displayed that Roister again thinks of going. This time he does depart, and is bidden to send Philip along if he should meet him. Tosspot remains, and when Philip has come to help Hance away (who is by now in a chair asleep), Tosspot accompanies them. "They three are gone togither, and Nichole newfangle remaineth behinde, but he must not speak til they be within"; for Hance and Philip are soon to return as Pickpurse and Cutpurse, and time is valuable. Alone on stage, Newfangle fights the delaying action with song and dance:

> And now I wil daunce, now wil I praunce,
> For why I haue none other woork:
> Snip snap Butter is no bone meat:
> Knaues flesh is no Porke (*etc.*)

He also takes this opportunity of telling the audience how he means to reward Tosspot and Roister (with the staff, wallet, and bottle proper to beggars), and so the action is advanced.

Not only in this interlude, but in general, the vice becomes the hub of the action. It seems probable that the doubling of parts enlarged the number of his soliloquies, as here in *Like will to Like*. He is prominent for two reasons. In the first place, he is usually the engineer of the events and a commentator on them. In the second place, he is the principal comedian. His monologues both inform and divert the spectators. For example, in Wapull's *The Tide tarrieth No Man* Corage is at every man's elbow, encouraging the young married man and the courtier to borrow from the merchant, and encouraging the merchant to exploit their wants, and the intervals between these and like scenes are filled with his exultations addressed to the audience, or perhaps a long nonsense-speech, or a fight with his subordinate Hurtful Help "to prolong the time while Wantonnesse maketh her ready" (this actor is changing out of the costume of the merchant Greediness; he has forty-eight lines, together with the fight, in which to make this change). It is an exhausting part, even for the most resilient actor; Corage does not leave the stage for the first twenty pages; a moral monologue by a downtrodden Tenant is his first opportunity to do so, and a page later he is back again, remaining for another seven and a half pages, and so on. He even doubles another part (the Debtor, who has one short appearance, arrested at the merchant's suit), though it is usual for the vice's part to be an actor's full-time responsibility.

It would be easy to multiply instances where the vice's monologues both fill the intervals during which the other actors change their costumes, and also link together the developments of the action. A striking example may stand for the rest. It is from *The Trial of Treasure*, which treats of the contrast between the lives of Lust and Just. The vice is Inclination (man's natural inclination to sin), who conquers Lust's mind early in the play; but when he tempts Just, Just bridles him, and departs from the scene along with his companion Sapience. As soon as they are out of sight, Sapience begins changing for Lust, and Just begins padding himself for Greedygut, who is a "cowe bellied knaue" and represents Lust's miserly tendencies. Meanwhile Inclination is indulging in horseplay—

> We he, he, he, he, he, come alofte I saye,
> Beware the horse heles I auise you, stande away,
> The raine of my bridle is tied so shorte,
> That I cannot make you any more sporte . . .

—and foretelling that Lust will not allow him to remain bridled; after his monologue Greedygut comes running in, followed by Lust, who releases Inclination.

An interesting change in dramatic construction, coinciding with the prominence of the vice and with the doubling of several parts by the other actors, is perhaps partly the result of this management of the characters. Whereas the earlier Tudor interludes, such as *Youth* and *Hickscorner*, showed the virtuous and the wicked in personal and even physical conflict (Youth threatens Charity with his dagger), the later ones are inclined to divide sheep from goats and to introduce them as separate flocks. Even *The Trial of Treasure*, though it opens with a physical wrestling-bout between Just and Lust, and continues with Just's bridling of Inclination, develops into two parallel biographies: Just takes the virtuous path and converses with Trust, while Lust consorts with Treasure and is powerless to survive God's Visitation (who, it is reported, has already made trial of Just). These two contrasted characters never meet after their opening contest. Instead their scenes are juxtaposed, partly with the deliberate purpose of stressing their moral opposition, and partly because each has accumulated companions like himself, who must appear with him and who thereby engage the company's whole resources. In the same way, Virtuous Life, who is contrasted with the assorted pairs of evildoers in *Like will to Like*, goes through the play without having anything to do with them; and the Heavenly Man in *Enough is as good as a Feast*, though he tries at the beginning of the play to reclaim the Wordly Man, almost drops out of sight during the sinner's progress to damnation, though he reappears to share in the epilogue.

Some deductions may be made about acting style when it is considered that only the vice could normally rely on having a single part, and that the other actors had to be able to combine at need the most grotesque assortments of characters. Indeed, the necessity to combine such diverse characters was thrust upon them by the alternation of scenes between the good and the evil groups. The distribution of rôles in *Enough is as good as a Feast* is representative:

1. Worldly Man.
2. Prologue, Heavenly Man.
3. Contentation, Temerity, Ignorance, Satan.
4. Enough, Hireling.
5. Inconsideration, Servant, Rest, Prophet.

6. Precipitation, Tenant, God's Plague, Physician.
7. Covetous (the vice).

From this distribution it is clear that, though typical social characters appear more and more often in Elizabethan interludes, this development was not accompanied by what is now called "type-casting." Hamlet's welcome to the players with his singling-out of "He that playes the King," "the Louer," "the humorous man," and so forth, cannot therefore be taken to imply that the members of small professional adult companies specialized in this way. (There is usually an attempt on the title-pages, however, to give one actor all the female rôles, where this is possible.) On the contrary, an actor might expect to play any combination of parts—a good man, a bad man, a rustic, a youth, an old man, even an old woman—and to be in alternate scenes of the same play a devil and an angel. The technique of acting must accordingly have been conventional and formal, so that the same actor was not instantly recognizable in all his parts. To a certain extent the developing decorum of style made this easier for him: the virtuous characters of William Wager's interludes have a noticeable tendency to rhyme-royal and to latinate rhymes, while his vicious characters employ a more racy and proverbial speech and are inclined to couplets or quatrains, and some "characters" (in the modern stage sense of the word) speak in stage-rustic after the manner of *Gammer Gurton's Needle*: "Enter an olde man Tenant and speake Cotesolde speech." Even so, something in the way of formalized speech and gesture would be desirable if the same actor were to be completely accepted as various characters.

Such a formal acting style is made the more necessary when parts are not doubled but halved; that is, when a scene so heavily taxes the company's resources that an actor must briefly take on a part that another actor has played in the rest of the performance. This practice, of which examples are recorded in the manuscript of those miracle plays genuinely belonging to Coventry,[24] is found at the end of *Three Ladies of London*. The three ladies, Lucre, Love, and Conscience, have all grown wicked, and are now brought to trial and sentenced to Hell. The judge bids the constable Diligence take Lucre away and bring forth Love, and there follows the direction "Let Lucar make ready for Loue quickly, and come with Dilligence." This direction, like those in *Enough is as good as a Feast* mentioned earlier, immediately follows the marked exit of the character concerned; and the actor making the change reappears as Love eighteen lines later. It is evident that, though Love's appearance here is a short one, and the whole scene could be played in tears (thereby further disguising the substituted actor), an acting style is wanted which is common to both players.

The boys' companies, with their larger number of actors, were in a different situation from that of the small troupe of five or six. Being under little or no necessity to double their main parts, they could specialize in particular kinds of rôle. In a graceful epitaph on the boy actor Solomon Pavy, Ben Jonson pays tribute to his celebrated acting of old men, which was so convincing that it deceived the Fates (the pretty conceit can be assumed to refer literally to a known speciality of this boy).[25] It seems likely that the boy actors of the Elizabethan interludes had already cultivated such arts; for though there is no solid evidence that particular boy actors specialized in this way, the conjecture is supported by the fact that most boys' plays contain scenes and speeches apparently designed to display these young actors' special talents.

There are many parts for which a boy actor would be the producer's obvious choice, and the authors of the boys' plays (unlike Lupton, writing presumably for men in *All for Money*) have not been sparing of boys and women among their characters. Besides the nine Muses in *Damon and Pithias*, there are Honest Recreation's women singers in *The Marriage of Wit and Science*, the singing maidservants in *Roister Doister*, and many others. The fact that a boy can not only look like a woman but also sing like one (which a man, unless he is a skilful counter-tenor, cannot even pretend to do) is exploited. So also is the levity natural to boys, particularly to precocious ones excited by the prospect of acting before the Queen at court. Thus the servants, both male and female, show signs of developing in these boys' plays towards the sprightly witty pages and servant-lasses of the plays of Lyly, where the boy actor enjoyed his heyday. The rise of decorum as a literary principle at this very time hastened the development. One of the greatest differences between Redford's *Wit and Science* (about 1540) and its anonymous successor *The Marriage of Wit and Science* (1567?), some thirty years later, is the prominence given to Wit's attendant Will, who appears only in the later play. Redford had given Wit servants of indeterminate age and courtly manners. His successor gives Wit an impetuous, energetic young page (the moral point that Will is not Wit's best counsellor is amusingly developed throughout the play). A characteristic exchange takes place between them on the way to Science's house, where Wit is to offer her his love:

WITTE: Perhappes we may fynd them at this time in bedde.
WILL: So much the rather loke you to be sped,
Care for no more, but once to come within her,
And when you haue done: then let another win her.
WITTE: To come within her child, what meanst thou by that.
WILL: One masse for a penye, you know what is what.
WITTE: Hard you euer such a counsell of suche a Jacke sprot.
WILL: Why sir do ye thinke to doe any good,
If ye stande in a corner like Roben hood . . .

The comedy here lies not only in Will's ribald suggestion, the knowing and anti-romantic grin of the rude boy, which is pointed by Wit's appeal to the audience when his Jack Sprat gives him this advice; it lies also in the fact that Wit himself is as young as this boy whose precocity shocks him so much. Wit gravely appeals to Elizabeth and her court as though he were their equal in years; and his own gravity increases their gaiety. I think it certain that this play (the courtly staging of which I discussed in the previous chapter) is the one recorded at court as *Wit and Will* —a title which aptly conveys the page's importance as a character.[26]

He is one of a number of lively boy-servants, others being Jenkin Careaway in *Jack Juggler*, Truepenny in *Roister Doister*, Mido and Ragau in *Jacob and Esau*, and Jack and Will (here short for William) in *Damon and Pithias*. All these are the active and unruly pages serving adult characters, and the fact that the cast in these plays is wholly composed of boys promotes the same kind of comedy as has just been illustrated from *The Marriage of Wit and Science*. In *Damon and Pithias*, for example, the old collier moralizes on the decadence and extravagance of modern youth, as represented by the two pages; and later in the scene he is shaved by them, while the audience must reflect that all three actors are alike beardless. Amusement is also obtained by the master's disciplining of the servant. In the opening scene of *Jacob and Esau*, Esau gives Ragau three strokes with his huntsman's whip; they are administered with conscious authority and received with absurd yells and howls. The amusement is closely connected with the fact that the actor of Esau is, in his own person, no less subject to such daily discipline. The scourging of Wit by Shame in *The Marriage of Wit and Science* (when the hero has been led astray by Idleness) is also ceremonious and amusing. Shame prefaces every blow with "A shame come to it"; and the contrite speech of Wit suggests how the audience is receiving the scene:

> Take ruthe and pittie on my playnt, or els I am forlorne,
> Let not the world continue thus, in laughing mee to scorne.

Besides the boy actor's nimbleness of body, liveliness of temperament, and sweetness of voice, another talent was at the dramatist's disposal: his power of mimicry, and of impersonation. Both boy-servants of *Jacob and Esau* indulge in imitation. At the very beginning of the play, Ragau "counterfaiteth how his maister calleth hym vp in the mornings, and of his answeres"; it is a monologue for two voices:

> For there is none other life with hym day by day,
> But vp Ragau, vp drousy hogges head I say:
> Why when? Up, will it not be? Up. I come anon.
> Up, or I shall reyse you in fayth ye drousy hooreson.
> Why when? shall I fette you? I come syr by and by.
> Up with a wilde wenyon, how long wilt thou lie? . . .(*etc.*)

Later, Mido (who has already imitated his blind master Isaac walking) vividly describes to Ragau how Esau greedily devoured Jacob's pottage:

> He woulde not haue a dishe, but take the pot and sup.
> Ye neuer sawe hungry dogge so slabbe potage vp.
> RAGAU: Why how did he suppe it? I pray thee tel me how?
> MIDO: Mary euen thus, as thou shalte see me doo now.
> Oh I thanke you Iacob: with all my hart Iacob.
> Gently done Iacob: A frendely parte Iacob . . .(*etc.*)

The direction here is "Here he counterfaiteth supping out of the potte," and the use of "counterfaiteth" on both these occasions makes it clear that a special piece of deliberate mimicry is involved. Burlesque gesture, here explicit, is implied in *Jack Juggler*, when Jenkin Careaway describes his fellow-servant the maid Alison Trip-and-go:

And a mayd we haue at hom aulsoon tripe and goo
Not all London shewe suche other twoo
She simperith, she prankith and getteth with out faille
As a pecocke that hath spred and sheweth hir gay taylle
She mynceth, she bridelethe, she swimmith to and fro
She tredith not one here a wrye, she tryppeth like a do
A brod in the stret going or cumming homward
She quauerith and warbelith like one in a galiard
Euerie ioint in her bodie and euerie part
Oh it is a ioylie wenche to myns and deuyd a fart . . .[27]

This speech acts itself, and would be impossible to recite without eloquent and indecorous swayings of the hips. It is interesting to reflect that, as Alison makes an appearance in the play, there must have been visible points of difference between the acting of the boy playing her and that of the boy playing Jenkin and (in that character) burlesquing her. The former would mimic a woman's walk with little or no extravagance; the latter would lard his mimicry with every imaginable affectation.

The singing ability of the boy actor, mentioned already, leads on to the use of music in the interludes. Though there are few of these plays which do not at some point introduce songs,[28] the songs are often unspecified and sometimes simply form a convenient method of closing an episode:

AVARICE: But sirs, because wee haue taried so longe:
If you bee good fellowes, let vs depart with a songe.
CRUELTIE: I am pleased, and therefore let euery man
Follow after in order as well as hee can.
The first song.[29]

In the boys' plays, however, the songs are seldom so informal; in *Apius and Virginia*, there is one trio for Virginia and her parents, and two trios for servants, the words in each instance being written out in full and forming an elaborate lyric with verses and a refrain. There are many other instances in all the plays likely to have been performed by boys—a trio in *Roister Doister*, another in *The Marriage of Wit and Science*, duets in *Patient Grissell* and *The Nice Wanton*, and so forth. The singing in *Patient Grissell* is important because it has an instrumental accompaniment ("Sound vp your Instrumentes"); and similarly in *Damon and Pithias*, "Pithias singes and the Regalles play."

As usual, one has often to guess, from the internal evidence, how much instrumental music was used in any given interlude and whether it was supplied by the actors or by musicians taking no other part in the play.[30] The statement on the title-page of John Rastell's *The Four Elements* that a disguising may be introduced "yf ye lyst" implies that an interlude might be decorated with music and dancing supplementary to the action; as it is, the music and dancing introduced into *The Four Elements* or into *Fulgens and Lucrece* have only the slightest connexion with the plot, and it looks as though the musicians and the dancers were specially enlisted for the performance. There seems to have been active collaboration between the professional musicians and the professional actors at court, as is illustrated by the casual requests for music in *Patient Grissell* and *Damon and Pithias*. In another boys' play, the marital farce *Tom Tyler and his Wife*, an accompanied song rounds off the action: "Here they all go in, and one cometh out, and singeth this Song following all alone with instruments, and all the rest within sing, between every staffe, the first two lines." In *Cambises* too, which may possibly have had a court performance (though by what kind of company, boy or adult, I cannot guess) the king demands that minstrels appear—"in place I would them spy"—and the direction "play at the banquet" suggests that they appear alongside the actors (though the doubling of the characters for eight actors does not allow for them). Earlier in this play, a lord, lady, and waiting-woman have played on lute and cittern, and when one takes into account the nearness of the audience it is hard to believe that these actors merely went through a mime of playing their instruments. I imagine that many actors had musical skill. Fulwell, planning a dance between the Devil and the Collier in his *Like will to Like*, relies on the vice's musical talents: "Nichol newfangle must haue a gittern or some other Instrument (if he may) but if they haue none they must daunce about the place all three, and sing this song that fulloweth, which must be doon though they haue an instrument." This elaborate rubric, though obviously addressed to the unknown company who will buy and act the play, leaves open the possibility that it had already been performed, that the vice had played on the gittern, and that Fulwell added the alternative direction when preparing the text for publication.

The demand for instrumental music implies either a well-organized performance (probably at court, college, or great house; travelling actors would hardly go to the expense of hiring musicians) or talented actors who were also musicians. The singers and dancers and musicians in *The Four Elements* and *Fulgens and Lucrece* illustrate the former situation; the latter is best seen in Redford's *Wit and Science*.

In *Wit and Science*, four of the performers are skilled instrumentalists, whose functions in the play have not (so far as I know) hitherto been traced. They make occasional exits, the sole object of which is to re-enter (sometimes after a change of costume) as a consort of viols. There is no statement in the text that doubling of the characters takes place, but analysis will show that the first of these four actor-musicians—or musician-actors—represents Confidence, Honest Recreation, and Fame; the second Study, Comfort, and Favour; the third, Diligence, Quickness, and Worship; and the fourth Instruction, Strength and Riches. (There are other possible distributions—Fame, Favour, Worship, and Riches appear in one scene only, and could be cast among these four actors in any way—but this does not alter the fact that all these twelve parts are divided among them.) The interlude requires at least eight actors altogether, since after Wit's victory over Tediousness there remain on stage Instruction, Wit, Study, and Diligence, who are joined by Science, Experience, Reason, and Confidence. There may have been more actors available; but if not, the four actors not playing viols—and here acting Wit, Science, Reason, and Experience—could easily combine the minor parts of Tediousness, Idleness, Ignorance, and Shame between them.

The first sign of this carefully-contrived doubling occurs during Wit's first (unsuccessful) combat with Tediousness. Instruction and Confidence are already off-stage, and are joined by Study and Diligence, who flee as Tediousness strikes Wit down. During Tediousness's boastful soliloquy they change their costumes, to reappear as Honest Recreation and her three singers, Comfort, Quickness, and Strength. At this point they only sing, for their hands are wanted in order to lift the prostrate Wit to his feet. Later in the scene, however, when Reason enters and begins to urge Wit not to neglect his enterprise of winning Science, there occur together the sudden marginal directions "al go out save honest recre." and "here comfort quiknes & strength go out"; for soon Honest Recreation will say "Go to my men play," at which point they presumably accompany Wit's dance on their viols. At the end of the dance, Wit sinks to sleep in the lap of Idleness, and Honest Recreation abandons him. Confidence enters seeking Wit, whom Idleness has by now left sleeping in a fool's coat, and (not finding him) goes out; and the next direction is "Here they cum in with vyoles," "they" being Fame, Favour, Worship, and Riches, the World's emissaries to Science, whom they serenade. There must have been a short pause before this entry, while Confidence jumped into his new costume and snatched up his viol. After Wit's final triumph, the betrothal song "Wellcum, myne owne" is apparently unaccompanied, like that of Honest Recreation and her singers; "& when the song is doone / reson sendyth instruccion / studye, and dyligence / & confidens out" without any words or indication of motive. This is in readiness for the final, self-accompanied song by them: "Heere cumth in fowre wyth violes & syng remembreance / & at the last quere all make cursye & so goe forth syngyng."

Some effort has clearly been made in this play to introduce more music than the action in itself requires, and to display the talents of the musicians. Whether these were called in for the occasion to take acting parts, or were actors with a musical bent, cannot be known. But this interlude establishes very firmly the active inter-relation between those court entertainers paid as musicians and those paid as actors. Like the payments to John Heywood the dramatist for singing and for playing on the virginals,[31] it shows how closely and delightfully music could be interwoven with drama in the early Tudor period.

Plate I. The Last Judgement

Plate II. The Prodigal giving a Banquet

Plate III. The Prodigal giving a Banquet

Plate IV. Prodigal Eating Husks

Plate V. Justice in the Stocks

Of Enuie.

{ While enuie seeketh to destroy : and will not cease to leaue hys will:
Then mischiefe most doth him annoy : and so of death he hath his fill.

The signification.

HE which striketh, with death behind him, signifieth enuiousnes against the quiet state of the faithfull, and in hoping by enuie to destroy, death is hys reward : the other by constāt faith in Christ is preserued, by the sword which is the word of God, and so ouercometh enuie : the Angell behind hym, is Gods prouident loue, which neuer faileth all those that trust in hym

H.j. The

PLATE VI. THE DEATH OF THE ENVIOUS MAN

Of Couetousnes.

Themistocles. { *It is better to haue men, hauing lacke of money, Then money hauing lacke of men.*

The signification.

THe Eliphant signifieth, force or strength: the mā on hys backe vsury: the Flag or banner in hys hand, signifieth illusion, or vaine hoped time: the Wolfe deuouring the lambe, signifieth all such gredy oppressours as do oppresse the poore and indigent: the cofer vnder hys arme Mammon: the purse destruction: and he which leadeth the Eliphant, is Nigardship: and the rope the which he is drawen withall, is deceate. Whē gredy death doth force assaile, and Nigardship begin to flie: thē pitie shall hys place possesse, & laud the name of God most hie.

A. Ni.

Plate VII. Usury Mounted on an Elephant

The description

Pythagoras. { *They which to slaunder or to kill,*
The dead haue their delight:

¶ *The signification.*

THe man which standeth lyke a Prophet signifieth godlines: the Fryer treason: the cup with the Serpent poyson: the other which striketh with the sworde murder: and he which is wounded is peace.

Nothing

PLATE VIII. A PROPHET, A FRIAR, AND A MURDERER

The trauailed Pilgrime

¶ The childe signifieth good Infancie: the rod, Correction: the auncient or aged man, Reason: the booke, Truth: the armed Knyght, youthfull Courage: the speare, good Gouernment: the shielde, Hope: the sword, Courage: standing in the fielde called Time.

Here the Author beginnes his voyage, being ready armed, bidding Infancie farewell, and now growing by Reason to further possibilitie and strength.

Plate IX. A Philosopher

The late ariuall,

Times past hath beene, as nowe to be seene.

Ezechiel, 4.	As wise as Serpents.
Esay. 3.	As suttle as Deuels.
Timothe. 3.	As craftie as Foxes.
Amos. 2.	As rauening as Wolues.

The long schull betokeneth Craftie imagination: The pleasant countenaunce, Flattery: The long necke, Excesse in eating and drinking: The right arme being shorter then the left, betokeneth small Deuotion: The bagge of money Couetousnesse: The left arme, Wilfulnesse: The sworde Crueltie: The straunge disguising in apparell, Pride

Plate X. A Satire on Gluttony, Pride, and Covetousness

PLATE XI. THE TRIUMPH OF PECUNIA

A lamentable tragedy

mixed ful of pleaſant mirth, conteyning the life of
CAMBISES **king of** *PERCIA*, **from the beginning**
of his kingdome vnto his death, his one good deed of ex-
ecution, after that many wicked deeds
and tirannous murders, committed by and
through him, and laſt of all, his odious
death by Gods Iuſtice appoin-
ted. Don in ſuch order as
foloweth. By
Thomas Preſton.

The diuiſion of the partes.

Parts		Parts	
Councel. Huf. Praxaſpes. Murder. Lob, the 3. Lord.	*For one man.*	Prologue. Siſamnes. Diligence. Crueltie. Hob. Preparatio the 1. Lord.	*For one man*
Lord. Ruf, Commons cry, Cõmõs cõplaint, Lord ſmirdis, Venus.	*For one man.*	Ambidexter Triall.	*For one man.*
Knight, Snuf. Small habilitie. Proof. Execution. Attendance. ſecond Lord.	*For one man.*	Meretrix. Shame. Otian. Mother. Lady. Queene.	*For one man.*
Cambiſes. Epilogus.	*For one man.*	Yung childe Cupid.	*For one man*

Plate XII. The Title Page of an Interlude, showing detailed Instructions for the Doubling of Parts

CHAPTER III

DRESS

IN the previous chapters I have suggested how intimate was the relationship established between the actors and the spectators when an interlude was performed. In order to persuade the spectators that everything they see is happening in the immediate present, the actors are usually dressed like the spectators. This dress serves as a reminder that the play deals with topical and particular aspects of general morality.

The meaning of costume had to be unequivocal when, among the smaller troupes at least, one man played many parts. The audience had to recognize the character, not the actor, and consequently the actor needed a peculiar and distinctive costume for each rôle if his several assumed personalities were not to become confused. Moreover, travelling actors must have adapted their limited wardrobe to their whole repertory. Companies playing at court could, it is true, draw upon the Revels Office for newly-devised costumes when their plays required them, and could also have the use of the "serviceable" garments preserved from past performances; but the greater the range of costumes, the more easy it would be to give the characters dresses appropriate to their natures.

In spite of the significance which might be given to contemporary dress, the actors were not restricted to it. Not every abstraction, clearly, can be represented as some social type. Truth, for example, preserved her traditional, distinctive white robe, though Simplicity, Honesty, or Plain Dealing could be (and were) incarnated as countrymen (in *Three Ladies of London*, *A Knack to know a Knave*, and Dekker's *The Whore of Babylon*). The appearance of other, new, abstract figures—Money and London and Tediousness—had to be specially devised by the authors of the plays in which they first appeared. The costumes of such figures afforded opportunities for originality and splendour which the dress of social types, heightened though it might be for stage effectiveness, could not provide. Ultimately, in the Jacobean masque, so much emphasis came to be laid on exotic decorative costume that it aroused the indignation of Jonson, whose upbringing was in the tradition of English moral and social comedy represented by the Tudor interludes, where the decorative quality of costume is not allowed to obscure its significance.[1]

An account of the costumes used in the interludes must begin with those of supernatural characters who were still appearing in the miracles—God, Satan, devils, and angels—and their immediate derivatives the angel-virtues and tormentor-devils of the interludes. Tudor clerical and secular dress will then be discussed; and last of all, costumes peculiar to pictorial and dramatic allegory.

Though the moral interludes continue to postulate an avenging and rewarding deity, the character of God ceases to appear after the plays of Henry VIII's reign, and in those early plays little can be deduced about the costume required. In the miracles God might be dressed either in rich clerical vestments or in the robes of an emperor, holding in either case an orb and sceptre as symbols of power. In the non-controversial plays *The Castle of Perseverance* and *Everyman*, either costume would serve, but by the time of Bale's plays God has become a Lutheran partisan, and the vestments of Rome are reserved to a very different use. In *Three Laws*, where this is particularly evident, God's opening line is "I am Deus pater, a substaunce inuysyble," but since this obviously refers to God as a Spirit, there is no reason to believe that the imperial robes were not worn: they would be especially suited to Bale's constant theme, the downfall of seditious plotters against their secular and spiritual head. (A German woodcut contemporary with Bale's plays shows a Deus Pater who might well have appeared in them; Plate I.)[2]

Satan, unlike God, makes more and more appearances in the interludes, always "as deformedly dressed as may be" (*All for Money*), his body covered in leather skins, or in a hairy pelt, or in feathers. When Sir Thomas More writes of "the rugged beare the deuyll," he is probably thinking of these costumes; and in *Like will to Like* Satan is compared by the vice to "Tom tumbler or els some dauncing beare" and is so grotesque that he has to be labelled: "This name Lucifer, must be written on his back and on his brest." Shakespeare is perhaps referring to such a practice when he makes Angelo exclaim in *Measure for Measure*:

> Let's write good Angell on the Deuills horne
> 'Tis not the Deuills Crest.

An important characteristic is an ugly nose, large and misshapen —he swears by his crooked snout in the Newcastle miracle of *Noah*—and in some interludes the vice ridicules it, saluting him in *Like will to Like* as "bottel nosed godfather" and "bottle nosed knaue," in *All for Money* as "bottell nosed knaue" and in *Susanna* as "crookte nose knaue." In *The Disobedient Child* the ugly feature is glanced at when the author makes Satan congratulate himself on his cleverness in the ironical phrase "this well fauoured heade of myne." This established tradition is still flourishing in *Wily Beguiled* (1606), where a character about to impersonate the devil promises:

> Ile put me on my great carnation nose
> And wrap me in a rowsing Calueskin suit.[3]

Accordingly, when Ithamore says gleefully in *The Jew of Malta*:

> I haue the brauest, grauest, secret, subtil, bottle-nos'd knaue to my Master, that euer Gentleman had,

I think that Marlowe is not only deriding his villain for having a Jewish nose but also condemning him as a devil. The sinister-comic relationship between Barabas and Ithamore certainly recalls the tradition, developed in some of the plays just mentioned, of a vice who both assists and mocks the devil.[4]

Minor devils also appear, though far less frequently than Satan. (They are quite distinct from the vice, whose dress will be discussed at the end of this chapter.) Mutes dressed as "*demones*" appear in *Wisdom* (late fifteenth century). In *All for Money* Lupton introduces, along with "Satan the great deuill," his sons Gluttony and Pride "dressed in deuils apparel," though in the second half of the sixteenth century, to which period this play belongs, it is unusual to find the Deadly Sins in devil form. They appear thus because Lupton is concerned to show the hellish affinity between devils and worldly evildoers, and it is to the worldly wicked that he has given the contemporary dresses of judges, merchants, landowners, and the like. Infidelity in *Three Laws* and the characters modelled on him in *King Darius* and *Mary Magdalene* (Iniquity and Infidelity) are denounced as fiends, but each is clearly nothing more than the disreputable comic vice of the play. (It is worth noting that whereas the vice's language is always jocular and usually obscene, the devil's is neither of these.) More properly considered as devils are those who tempt sinners to despair and suicide as the foul fiend has tempted Poor Tom in *King Lear*. When Despair and Mischief fail to persuade the ruined prodigal prince to use the suicide's traditional rope and dagger, in *Magnificence*, they take flight with hellish cries of "Out harowe! hyll burneth!" In *The Tide tarrieth No Man* Despair "in some ougly shape" tempts the young Wastefulness but is put to flight by his repentance; and again, in the German version of a lost English prodigal-son play, the ruined hero is offered a drawn sword by a character referred to variously as Despair and as Satan.[5]

The ugly masks worn by devils were worn also by the characters embodying God's judgments in the plays of Thomas Lupton and William and Lewis Wager. This is not surprising, since all these dramatists insist on God's dreadful power. In *All for Money*, Damnation the child of Sin "shal haue a terrible vysard on his face, & his garment shalbe painted with flames of fire," while God's Judgment and Confusion in *The longer thou livest the more Fool thou art* wear respectively "a terrible visure" and "an ill fauoured visure, & all thinges beside ill fauoured." Knowledge-of-Sin denounces the sinner in Lewis Wager's *Mary Magdalene* and terrifies her with his horrible appearance, while the vice calls him more "euill fauoured" than the devil and greets him with the customary "you bottell nosed knaue." In *The Trial of Treasure* the vice calls God's Visitation "you ilfauoured lowte"; the corresponding character in *Enough is as good as a Feast*, God's Plague, is not described, for he afflicts Worldly Man during the vice's absence, but he is doubtless of similar appearance.[6]

Along with the devils may be considered the souls of the damned. In *All for Money* "Iudas commeth in like a damned soule, in blacke painted with flames of fire, and with a fearfull vizard." The phrase "like a damned soule" indicates that the costume is traditional, and perhaps the point of Lupton's further details is that he preferred realistically painted flames to the stylized *appliqué* work suggested by the ten ells of black buckram and nine ells of yellow buckram which combined to clothe the "blake sollys" at Coventry in 1556. Whether the vizard was expressive of terror or was designed to terrify the spectators is not clear.[7]

In Redford's *Wit and Science* Tediousness is called "the feend" and has "a vyser over hys hed," this false head being brought in (like Macbeth's) by his triumphant slayer. He also carries a club. But though a club was sometimes the weapon of devils in miracles and folk plays, Tediousness is certainly not a devil but a savage giant. In a court disguising of 1515 there "sodainly came oute of a place lyke a wood .viij. wyldemen, all apparayled in grene mosse, made with slyued sylke, with Vggly weapons and terrible visages," to be driven out by as many knights, which seems akin to the romantic giant-killing plot of Redford's interlude. In the sixteenth century the word "fiend" was still used to signify a monster, as is clear from Redford's play and its derivatives *The Marriage of Wit and Science* (where Tediousness is a "monstrous Giant") and *The Marriage of Wit and Wisdom* (where Irksomeness enters "like a monstor"). In all three plays he has a false head. It should here be noted that the specified use of vizards and false heads in the Tudor interludes is limited to these examples and one other which I shall discuss later (Love's double face in *Three Ladies of London*).[8]

Costumes of angels play a prominent part in the miracles and may accordingly have seen service too in the interludes. The coat, wings, and yellow silk hair of an angel were among the properties of Queens' College, Cambridge, and were listed among the bursarial accounts some time between 1549 and 1555. Some angels are introduced ministering to Christ at the end of Bale's controversial *The Temptation of Our Lord*; and at the beginning of *Three Lords and Three Ladies of London* four angels, carrying "bright Rapiers" in their hands to indicate the defeat of the Armada (an event later symbolized in the action), escort London, the opening line of whose prologue is "Lo Gentles, thus the Lord dooth London guard." Like God, angels as heavenly beings do not often appear, but the costume also served to clothe virtues, such as the female Chastitie and the male Divyne Correctioun in Lyndsay's *Ane Satyre of the Thrie Estaitis*; and Peace, Justice, Verity, and Mercy, the four "ladies celestiall" who help to expose the frauds of Avarice and his fellows in *Respublica*, may also have worn this dress.[9]

The costume of virtues was not, however, always the angel's.

Latimer in a sermon personifies Faith as "a great state, a Ladye, a Dutches, a great womanne," and a German woodcut (Plate I) gives Peace, Justice, Verity, and Mercy a secular costume rich without extravagance, such as Latimer probably had in mind; in 1573 six virtues were costumed as "ladies" carrying lights for a court masque which was not in fact performed; and in a lost court play against Luther in 1527 the civil virtues Peace, Quietness, and Tranquillity were "rychely besyen in ladyes apparell." But fine apparel was not always for the virtues, and in *The Trial of Treasure* the author enforces an ascetic moral by denouncing Treasure ("a woman, finely appareled") through a visual contrast with Trust ("a woman playnly" [appareled]).[10]

In France, where most abstract nouns are of feminine gender, it was usual to represent the virtues as women. But apart from the Four Daughters of God in *Respublica* and Chastitie and Veritie in *Ane Satyre of the Thrie Estaitis*—for "truth is a shee, and so alwaies painted," as Lyly points out in *Sapho and Phao*—the interludes normally presented them as men. They were dressed either in the robes of holy orders or in some reverend garment such as the Prophet's or the Philosopher's. It is necessary to disregard completely the labelled woodcuts on early Tudor interludes' title-pages, such as those of *Hickscorner* and *Youth*, which are merely stock ornamental irrelevances, showing virtues wearing anything from commonplace Tudor dress to armour. The publishers preferred unsuitable decoration to no decoration at all. On the other hand, the illustrations to Stephen Batman's moral allegories *The Trauayled Pylgrime* and *A Christall Glasse of Christian Reformation* (both 1569) were specially designed to accompany a text which is clearly akin in spirit to the moral interludes, and they therefore provide more reliable evidence about costume. (Plates VIII and IX illustrate Batman's conception of a prophet and a philosopher.)[11]

A prophet's costume, comprising a gown of "tawny tilsent" (tawny tinsel, a tawny material interwoven with imitation gold or silver thread) and a cap of the same, is listed in the Losely MSS. among the properties for Edward VI's coronation plays, and sages in a court masque of 1574 wore "long gownes of Cownterfet cloth of golde &c."[12] When the ridiculous hero of *The Cobbler's Prophecy* is equipped by Mercury with "a prophets sute" and sent forth to denounce a decadent society, he evidently wears such a flowing robe, for he later remarks that his "vestment" is liable to catch fire should masquers come near him with torches. At the beginning of *All for Money* there enters Theology "in a long ancient garment like a Prophet" to talk with Science "clothed like a Philosopher"; and this assumes a recognizable difference between the costumes, evidently indicated in the word "ancient," which suggests an attempt at Hebrew garb for Theology and perhaps the contemporary form of academic dress for Science. The black gown of the younger scholar figures in Redford's *Wit and Science* where the young hero wears "garmentes of Science" on his back, and later loses his gown when dallying with Idleness. There are "sages" in *Three Lords and Three Ladies of London* to minister to the repentant Ladies at the beginning of the play; and Edification and God's Felicity, the "sages" of *New Custom*, must be distinguishable by costume both from the Papists and the Genevans, with whose vestarian conflict the play is partly concerned (the costume of Assurance in the same interlude is perhaps different again, since he is not called a sage but "a Vertue"). A "philosopher" speaks the epilogue of *Gentleness and Nobility* and a "doctor" that of *Everyman*; and this use of a costume clearly associated with age and dignity may have been customary in prologues and epilogues.

In the earliest moral interludes the virtues are men in clerical dress, as in the fifteenth-century *Mankind*, where Mercy gives "gostly solace" to the hero and is ridiculed by the evil-livers for his clerical Latin. Conscience is a friar in *Mundus et Infans*; he calls himself a "techer of the spyrytualete" and Manhood abuses him as "false flaterynge frere." In *Hickscorner* the dissolute Freewill derides Perseverance:

> What whome haue we here
> A preest a douctoure or elles a frere
> What mayster doctour dotypoll
> Can not you preche well in a blacke boll
> Or dyspute ony dyuynyte.

In *Youth*, Charity is scornfully hailed by Riot as "syr Iohn," and though this could be merely in derision of his moral speeches, the later action suggests that he is a cleric indeed.[13] The personal charges of simony and greed brought against Conscience by the usurer in *Impatient Poverty*, though clearly false, imply that he is in orders, especially as Envy in the same play taxes "the spyritualtye" in general with these same sins. For some years before this Edwardian play, however, controversy had led to a satirical use of the clerical costume in Protestant plays; and, as a result, virtues came to be dressed non-controversially as "sages," in *New Custom*, for instance, where independent "virtues" are introduced to approve the Genevans and instruct the repentant Papists.

Both Protestants and Catholics meanwhile dressed the cardinal virtues like themselves and the deadly sins like their opponents. A lost play against Luther, given at court in 1527, introduced Religion, Ecclesia, and Verity dressed as religious novices; but at the end of Bale's *Three Laws* are the following instructions:

Lete Idolatry be decked lyke an olde wytche, Sodomy lyke a monke of all sectes, Ambycyon lyke a byshop, Couetousnesse lyke a pharyse or spyrituall lawer, false doctrine, lyke a popysh doctour, and hypocresy lyke a graye fryre. The rest of the partes are easye enough to coniecture.

To catalogue every instance of this between Bale's plays and the end of the century would be tedious, but it can be truthfully said that scarcely a single anti-Catholic play in this period fails to introduce some such character as Flattery disguised as a friar (*Ane Satyre of the Thrie Estaitis*) or Ignorance as an old Popish priest (*Enough is as good as a Feast*, *The longer thou livest the more Fool thou art*, *New Custom*).[14]

From the bitterness of theological controversy it is a relief to turn to the non-controversial use of secular dress in the interludes. At the head of society comes the king, dressed as richly as may be. In *Wisdom*, Christ (or Wisdom) wears purple, cloth of gold and ermine, and has a crown, orb, and sceptre. This costume, which I think also clothed God in Bale's plays, here represents absolute worth and majesty. But in *The Castle of Perseverance*, *Mundus et Infans*, and *Nature* it is put to ambiguous use, for it is worn by the World, who bestows wealth and power on Man—worldly gifts which bring temptations. In plays with a political moral, *Magnificence* and *Ane Satyre of the Thrie Estaitis*, the costume implies the office of a reigning king. Though Lyndsay's king has the title of Humanitie, it is his practical function to call a parliament and redress the national wrongs.

Lords, besides attending on historical kings (*Cambises*), can have a symbolic function. In *Three Lords and Three Ladies of London* the lords are Policy "attired in blacke," Pomp "in riche roabes," and Pleasure "in collours"; these costumes distinguish the civic virtues which make London the nonpareil that the author claims her to be. A spectator's account, in 1540, of the first version of *Ane Satyre of the Thrie Estaitis* describes Temporalitie as "a man armed in harnes with a sword drawen in his hand," this indicating the power of the nobility.[15] The Knight in *Gentleness and Nobility* (another play presenting a conflict of estates) may also have worn armour, for he claims pre-eminence because he defends the realm; and his being beaten by the aggressive Ploughman would be particularly ludicrous if he were wearing armour.

Scarlet robes are worn by the Elders (or "Iudges") in *Susanna*, where the vice calls them "bloody gownes" more than once, implying the cruelty of the wearers. Scarlet was probably worn also by the judges in *All for Money*, *Cambises*, and *Like will to Like*. In the last of these, the judge Severity carries a sword when he enters to sentence Cutpurse and Pickpurse to death; and the sword is also carried by Justice in *Apius and Virginia* and by the Last Judgment (an old man in red) in *The Cradle of Security*, a play of which only a report survives.[16]

From these official costumes we next turn to the private dress of social groups. The most evident contrast sought was one between age and youth, where a moral purpose combined with a desire to observe decorum:

> for youth no less becomes
> The light and careless livery that it wears
> Than settled age his sables and his weeds,
> Importing health and graveness.[17]

The purpose of most moral interludes is to condemn the extravagance and frivolity of the young "gallant." His dress, intended by him to reach heights of novelty, became for that reason as instantly identifiable as a uniform. When sumptuary laws prevented, or at least condemned, excesses in apparel, it would be instantly perceived that a character in a feathered hat, slashed doublet, scalloped sleeves, and (later) bombasted breeches was full of vanity and wickedness: "Thou lookst like *Antichrist*, in that lewd hat."[18] Thus, in *Lusty Juventus*, Good Counsel blames the hero : "To aduaunce your flesh, you cut and iag your clothes"; and the ascetic Just in *The Trial of Treasure* coldly distinguishes himself from Lust the voluptuary, who has entered "like a gallant":

> Myne apparell is not like vnto thyne,
> Disguysed and iagged of sundrie fashion,
> Howe be it, it is not golde alwayes that doth shine,
> But corrupting Copper of small valuation.[19]

In *Like will to Like* the direction "Tom Tospot commeth in with a fether in his Hat" announces him as a debauched prodigal; from this one detail the producer would know the rest of the costume required by Tom Tosspot and his companion Rafe Roister. The vice, Nichol Newfangle, says to Tosspot "Methink by your apparell you haue had me in regard." Newfangle's mission, as his opening soliloquy makes clear, is to devise extravagant fashions, "And especially Breeches as big as good barrels." This fashion is glanced at also in *Damon and Pithias*, where the pages' wide breeches are to the moralizing collier signs that they will be hanged; and it is illustrated by Stephen Batman in 1573 (Plate X).

The prodigal was always extravagantly dressed; even when there is no explicit stage direction this can be deduced from remarks like the father's complaint in *The Disobedient Child* that parents labour to make their children "goe tricksie, gallaunt and cleane," or the over-indulgent mother's reply in *The Nice Wanton* when a neighbour warns her about her children: "Because they go handsomly, ye disdayne." Sometimes the costume reveals aspects of the character which are only hinted at in the text. Medwall's *Fulgens and Lucrece* deals with the theme of virtue as the true nobility, its subject being the rivalry in wooing between Flaminius (a man of virtue but undistinguished birth) and Cornelius (a wealthy patrician). The latter's servant, early in the play, describes his master's finery, adding that his inherited wealth is such that he "lassheth it forth daily." He goes on to praise this as liberality and an encouragement to trade, but Medwall's attitude appears from the fact that the costume described—striped hose, a vast codpiece, a gown both short and full—combines features similar to those of Pride and of the degenerate Man in his other play, *Nature*. Accordingly the force of the tribute:

> Many a pore man therby doth wyn
> The chef substauns of hys lyuing

is ironical. The gallant's costume continues on the Elizabethan public stage, and indicates (for example) the degeneracy of Gaveston in *Edward II* or of Richard II's favourites in *Woodstock*; it also, I imagine, distinguishes the decadent "barber-monger" Oswald from the homespun plain-dealing Kent (as Caius) in *King Lear*.

There was an equivalent costume for female characters, described in detail in Lewis Wager's *Mary Magdalene*, where Pride instructs the heroine:

> Vpon your forhead you must weare a bon grace,
> Which like a penthouse may com farre ouer your face,
> And an other from your nose vnto your throte,
> Of veluet at the least, without spot or moate.

Pride also dictates elaborate hair dressing, tight-laced stays, and hooped skirts. Mary adopts this costume and the worldly code of conduct appropriate to it, but after her conversion to virtue reappears "sadly apparelled." When a kirtle of silk is discovered beneath the habit of the Prioress in *Ane Satyre of the Thrie Estaitis* everybody identifies her as "ane cow-clink" (prostitute), and these associations of finery with debauchery are developed allegorically in *The Trial of Treasure*, where "Treasure, a woman, finely appareled" represents the meretricious lure of money.

The evident prosperity of the virtuous rich man is different from the reckless self-adornment of the gallant. The father of the prodigal in *The Disobedient Child* is constantly referred to in the directions as the Rich Man. His unspecified costume must represent an enduring contrast to both those of his son, who is at first extravagantly, and at last poorly, dressed. In *Enough is as good as a Feast*, when the vice is about to tempt Worldly Man, he hastily sends for his cap, gown, and chain; and then, having made himself respectable and assumed the name of Policy, he recommends avarice and extortion. When he next meets Worldly Man, the latter is in the company of "poorly arayed Inough," and there is a piquant contrast of costume between Enough and Covetous the vice.

Some unmistakable signs usually distinguish the wealthy extortioner from the virtuous rich man. Nichol-never-out-of-law, in *All for Money*, enters to buy justice "like a riche frankeline, with a long bagge of bookes by his side," the books expressing the fondness for unjust litigation whereby he ruins his poorer neighbours; the greedy miser Money-without-Learning in the same play is "apparelled like a riche churle, with bagges of money by his sides." On the Tudor stage, avarice is so constantly identified with extortionate and selfish prosperity that the hoarder, instead of being represented traditionally as a thin starved creature, is shown usually as a gluttonous profiteer, bloated with ill-gotten gains and carrying about his moneybags and coffers on his person (like Usury in Stephen Batman's picture, Plate VII).[20] In *Respublica*, Avarice, "the vice of the plaie," has purses continually hanging at his back, though concealed under his gown during most of the action, and at last he is sentenced to be pressed like a sponge to empty him of the wealth he has absorbed. The covetous yeoman Tenacity in *Liberality and Prodigality* complains that he has made a long journey to Fortune's palace:

> Cham sure chaue come, vorty miles and twenty,
> With all these bags you see, and wallets empty.

He is old, crusty and ponderous: Vanity, Fortune's steward, calls him "father Croust," and he is also described as

> a lubber, fat, great, and tall,
> Vpon a tyred asse, bare, short, and small

—the "beggers state" for which Vanity rebukes him, referring to his equipage and not to his costume, which perhaps included a furred hood, another mark of the stage usurer.[21] Another covetous rustic, Greedygut in *The Trial of Treasure*, who bids the evildoer Lust "Eat vp at a mouthfull, houses and landes," is derided by the vice as "old knaue," "cowe bellied knaue," and "great bellied loute." It is an accepted convention that the hoarder has a glutton's figure. Falstaff, playing the highwayman at Gadshill, invokes this convention when he denounces his victims as "gorbellied knaues" and "fat chuffs" and sees himself as a vigorous young prodigal driven to robbery like Ismael in *The Nice Wanton* and Prodigality in *Liberality and Prodigality* ("They hate vs youth"; "Yong men must liue"); and the comedy springs from the unsuitability of Falstaff's theatrical *clichés*, which draw attention to his own age and corpulence.

The prodigal gallant is frequently reduced to beggary. ("With Dye and drab, I purchas'd this Caparison.")[22] In *The Nice Wanton*, where Ismael her brother becomes a highway robber and is hanged, Dalila becomes a prostitute and "commeth in ragged, her face hid, or disfigured, haltinge on a staffe." The hero of *The Disobedient Child*, reduced to poverty by his imprudent marriage, laments:

> That now I am fayne, a Cote that is rent
> Alas to weare for verye shame.

In *Lusty Juventus*, the prodigal spurns Good Counsel's reproaches in a phrase suggesting the beggary that follows gaming:

> What hast thou to do, and if I loose my cote,
> I wyll trill the bones while I haue one grote.

This tradition seems to be followed in *Liberality and Prodigality*, where the abstract character Money, having escaped from Prodigality, enters shivering and in rags. Professional beggars carried the bag, bottle, and staff with which the dissipated and ruined Tosspot and Roister are presented by the vice in *Like will to Like* (each having "lost all that he hath, saue his Doublet and his Hose"); though they have lost their hats, the stage-direction insists that each must wear "a night Cap because the strings of the beards may not be seene." At the end of *Horestes*, when the hero's marriage has settled Amity in the land, the vice (Revenge), finding himself unemployed, "entrith with a staffe & a bottell or dyshe and wallet," and trudges resentfully off to seek his fortune in the service of women. Other plays make a similar allegorical use of the beggar's costume to clothe a quality which has either degenerated or gone out of request. Love, Lucre, and Conscience, the *Three Ladies of London*, are imprisoned in Hell at the end of the play for their misdeeds; and the sequel *Three Lords and Three Ladies of London* opens with their entry in the rags of repentance ("Ladies alas, what tattered soules are we?") to be clothed anew by Honest Industry, Pure Zeal, and Sincerity. Probably the mean garments in which Christ's Law is disfigured by the vices in Bale's *Three Laws* were the beggar's rags.[23]

In *Godly Queen Hester*, the extravagance of Aman beggars Pride himself, who enters "poorely arayed" to complain with Ambition and Adulation that Aman has ruined them all by engrossing their qualities to his own use. A further purpose of the beggar's costume and character is to bring out the worldliness of avaricious men. Thus in *All for Money* a beggar is employed to play Lazarus to the rich churl's Dives; this beggar, Neither-Money-nor-Learning, is refused alms by the extortioner Money-without-Learning, but granted them by the virtuous and prosperous scholar Learning-with-Money. A beggar with the similar function of testing the principles of the other characters for the audience's benefit appears in *A Knack to know a Knave*.

Last among the social types to be considered here is the "ruffian," or professional man of violence. Also known as the "ruffler," he is to be distinguished from the moneyless prodigal who has turned to casual robbery. A distinction is also to be made between the two sixteenth-century senses of "ruffler." The word means, in its more general sense, the same as "gallant" when that word is used, in a derogatory context, of a roistering and showily-dressed young man. But in its particular sense it means a discharged serving-man or soldier who has taken to robbery with violence, and who belongs (as a stage character) to the same social level as Pierce Pickpurse and Cuthbert Cutpurse in *Like will to Like*. One such character, Gregory Graceless, enters "like a ruffian" in *All for Money* and bribes the judge to dismiss the case against him. The equipment of the rôle is indicated in *Three Ladies of London* where Fraud comes in "with a sword and a Buckler like a Ruffian," and his principal scene in this play is his incitement of two beggars to rob a merchant. Sturdiness also, who is Lust's most aggressive supporter in *The Trial of Treasure*, and promises to uphold him by force in wrongful causes, was probably a swashbuckler. Treated comically, like Huff, Snuff, and Ruff in *Cambises*, Snatch and Catch in *The Marriage of Wit and Wisdom*, or the hero of *Thersites* (who has a "blacke and rustye gryme berde"), they are laughable; but they can be very sinister, like Cruelty and Murder, hired bravos "with bloody hands" in *Cambises*, or Cruelty and Avarice in *New Custom*, "rufflers" upon whose assistance the old popish priest Perverse Doctrine relies.

It will be noted that all these costumes of social types are capable of symbolic use, to clothe virtues and vices, and to suggest rapid and dramatic fluctuations in fortune. I shall return to these points in the next chapter, which will deal more fully with the significance of changes in costume.

For wholly abstract characters it became necessary to desert contemporary dress, and to design special costumes. Thus Lupton (in *All for Money*) can satirize corrupt justice in the person of the magistrate All for Money, but Money himself "commeth in, hauing the one halfe of his gowne yellowe, and the other white, hauing the coyne of siluer and golde painted vpon it." This prevents the confusion between abstract and concrete characters which would result were Money wearing any representative Tudor social costume; similarly (as I have said) Gluttony and Pride appear as devils because their contemporary exponents also appear in the play as extortioners and litigious landowners. In the revels accounts for the period November 1574–February 1575 a similar costume is indicated by such items as "a ffelt that was couered with mony," "syluer paper to make mony," and a payment "for stytching a Cote and a payer of Buskyns with a hatt made all ouer with syluer coyne and for silk for the same." It is very probable that these were used for Money's costume in the court play of *Liberality and Prodigality*.[24]

Fortune, who also appears in *Liberality and Prodigality*, was presumably always identifiable by her wheel. In Dekker's *Old Fortunatus* she is accompanied by nymphs who carry it and a globe to signify her power over things of this world. In the two Tudor moral interludes in which she appears, *Liberality and Prodigality* and *The longer thou livest the more Fool thou art*, she may well carry her attributes herself, as her part in the action involves little gesture, her main function being to influence events. In *The longer thou livest the more Fool thou art* she enters alone, and so must carry her wheel herself if she has it. The laboured description which Fluellen gives of her in *Henry V* depends for its comedy on the fact that everyone must have been perfectly familiar with all its details by means of pictures and the stage.[25] Whether she appeared on stage blindfolded, as Fluellen describes her, is not certain, but *Liberality and Prodigality* strongly suggests that she did: Liberality calls her "blind," and Prodigality abuses her as "thou abominable, blinde, foule filth." The fact that in this play she descends from her throne unaided, and nearly strangles Prodigality when he attempts to break into her palace, need not prevent her eyes from being lightly bandaged, for in Bale's *Three Laws* provision is made for Moses' Law, blindfolded by the vices, to walk on and off the stage by himself. There is also a possibility that, Janus-like, she wears a false face on the back of her head, and that Virtue's remark "She beares a double face, disguised, false, and fickle" is not merely metaphorical. Fortune was sometimes so represented in contemporary art,[26] and that the device was used in Elizabethan stage performance is plain from the direction in *Three Ladies of London* that when Love has married Dissimulation and changed her name and nature to Lust she must wear "a visard behind." Fortune's garments in *Liberality and Prodigality* are of great splendour—"vestures wrought with gold so gorgeously"—signifying her worldly glory and esteem and, with her stately throne, forming a strongly moral visual contrast with Virtue's sober dress and homely bower.

Time appears as a character only in one Tudor interlude, *The Trial of Treasure*, where (as Chronos) he performs the final destruction of Lust, a debauched worldling who has neither harkened to the advice of the godly Just nor been moved by the threats of God's Visitation. Time's costume here is not indicated, probably because his forelock, hourglass, and scythe were too familiar to need mention.[27]

Truth, the daughter of Time, who appears as one of the Four Daughters of God (with Peace, Justice, and Mercy) in *The Castle of Perseverance*, and the Marian *Respublica*, is represented in Protestant plays as Verity, carrying the New Testament in English translation. "Gods worde. A woman with a Bible in her arms" is listed among the characters of a lost interlude of Edward VI's court; a Verity with a Bible greeted Elizabeth at her coronation pageant in 1559.[28] In Lyndsay's *Satyre of the Thrie Estaitis* Veritie is indignantly challenged by Flatterie (who has dressed himself as a friar and is in league with the Roman Catholic clergy whom the play attacks):

> Quhat buik is that, harlot, into thy hand?
> Out walloway, this is the New Test'ment,
> In Englisch toung, and printit in England:
> Herisie, herisie, fire, fire, incontinent!

In the Jacobean play *The Whore of Babylon* (by Dekker) the clown Plain Dealing is at pains to distinguish between Truth, whom Titania (Elizabeth) serves, and Falsehood, whom Babylon (Rome) misrepresents as Truth. He asks Truth to prove that she is what she seems, and she replies that he may know her "because I am not painted." Like Hamlet, Plain Dealing has heard of women's paintings, and is jesting on the subject when Truth further explains:

My skins not spotted
With foule disease, as is that common harlot,
That baseborn trueth, that liues in Babylon;

and later in the play Falsehood appears with a red-spotted face. Spots, as will be seen in the next chapter, always signify moral corruption. Ill Fame is shown on the title-page of Ralegh's *History of the World* (1614) as a woman whose person and garments are spotted, and possibly these spots also appeared on the person and garments of Shame in *Cambises*, who enters with a black trumpet to noise abroad the king's wickedness. But there is little evidence to base conjecture upon. The rôle is given on the title-page to an actor who also plays four women and a youth, so it may be feminine, and the alliterative opening lines of Shame's speech—

From among the grisly ghosts I come, from tirants testy train;
Unseemly *Shame* of sooth I am—

are (like much of the verse in this play) so strongly influenced by English translations of Seneca's plays that "unseemly Shame" may have been represented as a Fury with snaky locks. Shame is masculine in *The Nice Wanton*, where he carries a knife and offers it to the despairing mother whose children have come to bad ends through her bad upbringing of them, and also in *Wit and Science* and *The Marriage of Wit and Science*; in the second of these plays he has a knife, but his function in both of them is to flog the neglectful Wit for his dalliance with Idleness. His garments are not specified in any of these three plays.[29]

The costume of Fame is easier to determine. She is consistently referred to as feminine except in *Like will to Like*, where her sex is unspecified (as this play ends with a song in which Fame joins, a boy may be presumed to have taken the part). At the beginning of *Three Ladies of London* Fame appears as a presenter sounding the golden trumpet traditionally associated with her; and she also carries the iron trumpet of denunciation in *Horestes*, where she has wings and a decorative costume ("trym geare" which the vice praises). In the revels accounts for the reign of Edward VI an item is "payntinge of a cote and a capp with Ies tonges and eares for fame"; and there is also listed a costume required for Edward VI's coronation plays, consisting of "a Coote Cappe and skabart of vellet whyte and grene Checkyd garnyshed with skaloppe shelles crosse keyes clothe of Syluer yes tonges & Eres"; these lost plays included some anti-Catholic touches (the bishop of Rome is listed among the characters) and the cross keys and scallop shell suggest that this costume may have been for a vicious character, Catholic False-Report for example.[30] Chaucer's account in *The House of Fame* had made these eyes, tongues and ears familiar, and they recur as decorative motifs when Report, "appareled in Crymosyn satyn full of tongues," is introduced into a court disguising of 1518, and when Rumour "painted full of tongues" delivers the prologue to *2 Henry IV*.[31] Another Rumour, equipped with a trumpet (like Fame and Shame), announces in *Patient Grissell* that Gautier has decided to reject Grissell and choose another bride.

It is possible that this device of covering a character's garments with symbolic motifs was a widespread one, at least in court plays. The revels accounts furnish another instance: "Labour, a woman with many hands" in a lost Edwardian play. We may assume that these hands were not model hands, but decorative hands sewn or painted all over the garment to signify manual labour, just as Money's coins or Fame's tongues are stitched or painted on their costumes.[32]

The costume of Vanity, Fortune's steward in *Liberality and Prodigality*, is covered with variously-coloured feathers to suggest frivolity. The revels accounts for 1574–75 describe a costume, evidently this one, as "A Cote, A hatt, & Buskins all ouer couered with fethers of cvllers for Vanytie in sabastians playe."[33] The character expounds the significance of his own costume:

> For lo, thus round about in feathers dight,
> Doth plainely figure mine inconstancie,
> As feathers, light of minde, of wit as light,
> Subiected still to mutabilitie.
> And for to paint me forth more properly,
> Behold each feather decked gorgeously,
> With colours strange in such varietie,
> As plainely pictures perfect Vanitie.

Whereas the symbolic use of particular colours is often capricious, not to say arbitrary, in the Tudor interludes, this multi-coloured costume almost always carries condemnation with it. It is the producer's responsibility in *Three Lords and Three Ladies of London* to make the costume of Lord Pleasure ("in collours") appear virtuous and not frivolous. The contrary effect is to be aimed at in *The Trial of Treasure*, where Pleasure is the younger brother of the extravagantly-dressed woman Treasure and both attend on the evil "gallant" Lust. The author makes a difficulty for himself here, however, for near the end of the play God's Visitation deprives Lust of Pleasure, saying that Pleasure "shall nowe attend on the Just," and as Just is an ascetic in clothing and morals a gaudily-dressed Pleasure would be an embarrassment to him; this the author seems to have recognized, since he never shows us Pleasure attending on the Just, whose virtue is rooted in self-denial, and whose joy is a contemplative tranquillity. In Bale's *King John*, diverse colours imply duplicity; Dissimulation wears a monk's habit, evidently of various hues which he points out to the admiring Sedition and to the audience:

> nay dowst thou not se, how I in my colours Iette?
> to blynd the peple, I haue yet a farther fette
> this is for bernard, & this is for benet
> this is for gylbard, & this is for Ihenet
> for frauncys this is, & this is for domynyke
> for Awsten, & elen, & this is for seynt partryk
> we haue many rewlles, but neuer one we kepe
> whan we syng full lowde, ower hartes be fast aslepe
> we resemble sayntes, In gray whyte blacke & blewe
> yet vnto prynces, not one of ower nomber trewe.[34]

Perhaps the habit worn by Sodomy (dressed like "a monke of all sectes" in *Three Laws*) was also multicoloured in this fashion. Another Dissimulation, appearing among Lucre's adherents in *Three Ladies of London*, is described on his first entrance as "hauing on a Farmers long coat, and a cappe, and his powle and beard painted motley," and he explains in cheerful rhymes that his "partie coloured head" signifies that his "honestie is fled" (the farmer's coat is a disguise whereby he hopes to pass as an honest man). In the sequel, *Three Lords and Three Ladies of London*, he continues to flaunt his "motley-beard" amid the disguises imposed on him in the play. Though Dr Hotson has shown that the "motley" of court and stage fools was often a dull speckled material of a dark greenish tinge rather than a brilliant particoloured one, it seems that the use of strongly contrasted colours is wanted here, in order to give proper prominence to the wig and beard. Perhaps a motley wig was frequently worn by the dissembling vice, for in Dekker's *Satiromastix* Captain Tucca scornfully says that Horace's ambition is "to bite euery Motley-head vice by'th nose."[35]

There seems also to have been a recognized use of parti-colour for parasites. An elegy lamenting Elizabeth's death yet welcoming James's succession, printed in the anthology *Sorrowes Joy* (1603), begins:

> Now is my Muse clad like a Parasite,
> In partie-coloured roabes of blacke and white;
> Grieving and ioying too, both these together;[36]

and "a parasites cote and hose" (not, unfortunately, described) is listed among the dramatic properties at Jesus College, Cambridge, in 1563–64, which points to this as a tradition of long standing. The few Tudor interludes containing characters called "parasites" (Carisophus the court pickthank in *Damon and Pithias*, and Common Conditions the comedian-servant in *Common Conditions*) do not specify their costumes.[37] It may not be relevant to English drama to mention a German engraving, but from those reproduced in Plates II and III, it appears that, in Europe at least, the stage parasite was sometimes clothed as a court-fool. The first illustration is a woodcut by Jörg Breu the Elder (1480–1537), depicting the prodigal son of the biblical parable. The second is a copy in reverse of this, with the dress of the characters modified in varying degrees, and the names of characters in *Acolastus* appropriately attached to them. *Acolastus*, a Latin play on the fall and repentance of a prodigal, was printed in 1529 and translated into English in 1539–40; it had a good deal of literary influence. The labelled picture shows Acolastus the prodigal and Lais the harlot, with Astyanassa and Sura (these two do not appear in the play) and Pamphagus and Pantolabus, the latter dressed in a fool's cap.[38] The closest approach to this in the Tudor drama is found in the Elizabethan play *Misogonus*, which like *Acolastus* deals with the reform of a prodigal and is constructed to some extent upon classical lines. The hero is encouraged by his father's knavish fool Cacurgus, "who for his simplicitie a fooles cote doth wear," and who talks of the long ears on his cap.

Though the costume of the fool clothes this comic figure in *Misogonus*, it would be most unwise to assume its general use in the Tudor interludes. I think the professional fool's costume (whether of motley as defined by Dr Hotson or parti-coloured) was recognizably distinct from the motley colours symbolically worn by the dissembler. Nor can I find any instance of the professional fool's costume clothing the vice.

Apart from a general working definition of "chief tempter and chief comedian" little can be said with certainty about the vice, though much has been conjectured. It is surprising that scarcely anything is known of the dress of a character who in different forms appears in most moral interludes, but that is the case. His evil disposition is usually insisted on—in only a few plays, *The Weather* and *Love* and *Jack Juggler*, do we find a merely amusing and not at all sinister figure listed as the vice—and he is occasionally a confederate of the Devil. As will be seen in the next chapter, he sometimes (though again, not always) disguises himself in order to tempt human sinners more effectively, and it can therefore be reasonably conjectured that his normal dress is not a dignified one. On the other hand, it can hardly be supposed that this normal costume was that of the fool, whose character was often associated with innocence and never with that gross worldly wisdom which the vice so eminently displays. And if the vice were dressed as a fool, what would be the costume of his associates and subordinates, of whom most Tudor moral interludes show two or three? Moreover, when the fool's dress is used in the interludes, it is used dramatically and surprisingly, for a specified purpose, as when the sleeping Wit is dressed as a fool by Idleness in Redford's *Wit and Science* or when Moros receives his deserved fool's-coat at the end of Wager's *The longer thou livest the more Fool thou art*. These incidents, and the unfrocking of the wicked clergy in *Ane Satyre of the Thrie Estaitis*, are discussed in the next chapter. The disguising of Flatterie, Falset, and Dissait in this last play should, however, be discussed now, since if any of them is dressed as a professional fool we have an instance invalidating my argument.

The first point of importance is that, though Flatterie's first speech lends some colour to the idea that he is dressed as a fool, that inference can be drawn about neither of his companions. And Flatterie's own words about himself are ambiguous:

> Mak roume sirs hoaw, that I may rin,
> Lo se quhair I am new cum in,
>   Begaryit all with sindrie hewis.

It is not even clear whether this refers to his costume (as is usually supposed) or to his person.[39] He may resemble the motley-bearded, motley-wigged Dissimulation of *Three Ladies of London*. And even if it does refer to his costume, the costume is not therefore established as that of the court-fool, for in Bale's *King John* the monk Dissimulation has jetted in his colours. Though he goes on to tell the audience that he is "Flatterie, your awin fuill," and says he was with them at Yule, this may be merely jocularity about his colourful appearance and clownish behaviour.[40] The sundry hues seem to be peculiar to Flatterie and to symbolize his super-excellent knavery (it is he who finally hangs his fellows).

To recommend themselves to King Humanitie in the first part of the play, the three rogues disguise themselves, Flatterie in the robes and cowl of a friar, and Falset and Dissait in "clarkis cleathing." Flatterie's companions cast away their disguises when they have stolen the king's treasure and are fleeing from Divyne Correctioun, and when they appear in the second part of the play they are still wearing their original clothes, though Flatterie retains his friar's habit.

The audience has thus become familiar with the dress of Flatterie and his fellows. Now if this dress were the fool's costume, the play's most dramatic visual effect would be anticipated and blunted: the unfrocking of the clergy, to reveal fool's coats beneath their robes. The spectators know that Flatterie (now also unfrocked) is disguised, and are prepared to see his real self emerge from beneath the friar's habit; but that the clergy are other than they seem has never been hinted, and the point of this unfrocking is not, surely, that they resemble Flatterie, but that they differ dramatically from what they seemed to be.

Moreover, a distinction (albeit a fine one) is drawn between these unfrocked clergy on the one hand and Flatterie and his fellows on the other. When the clergy's robes are removed, they can be seen by all as "verray fuillis," and the word "fuill" is bandied about some half-dozen times before they vanish. But nobody calls Flatterie or his fellows fools, even in abuse: "loun" and "lurden" (rogue, knave) are the words applied to them all. It is most probable, then, that they are dressed merely in some disreputable way, not in the special garments of the recognized fool.

This, I think, must also be the conclusion reached about other vices in the interludes. It is not until 1616 that we find Ben Jonson using "vice" as a synonym for "fool"—

> That's *fifty* yeeres agone, and *six*,
> (When euery great man had his *Vice* stand by him,
> In his long coat, shaking his wooden dagger)[41]

—and by Jonson's time the vice, as a stage character, had disappeared. It is easy enough to understand that, since the wicked characters in the drama offer most opportunities for eccentric comedy, the comedian might become known as the vice even though he were not vicious. It was also natural that the comic tempter should sometimes have comic equipment like the wooden dagger, or dagger of lath, mentioned by Jonson and Shakespeare;[42] Nichol Newfangle, the vice of *Like will to Like*, and Covetous, the vice of *Enough is as good as a Feast*, fight their associates absurdly with their daggers. But it must be made clear that the wooden dagger is given to these vices because it can be turned to comic use, not because it is their necessary and peculiar appurtenance.[43]

The essence of the vice's dress is its reckless disreputability. John Heywood's character Merry Report in *The Weather* (one of the first characters to be called "the vice" in the *dramatis personae*) is evidently unseemly in his dress, since when he calls himself a gentleman Jupiter disallows the claim:

> A gentleman thy selfe bryngeth wytnes naye
> Both in thy lyght behauiour and aray.

This phrase "light array" is developed at more length in Bale's *King John*, where Usurped Power is identified by Private Wealth as the Pope, and Sedition objects that he looks like a knave. In mitigation it is explained that "though he for his pleasure, soche lyght apparell haue" he is informally dressed because "yt is now sommer, & the heate ys withowt mesure." The best gloss on both passages is Skelton's description, in his poem *The Bowge of Court*, of Riot, a disreputable person met by the Dreamer, as

> A rusty gallande, to-ragged and to-rente; . . .
>
> His here was growen thorowe oute his hat . . .
>
> His gowne so shorte that it ne couer myghte
> His rumpe, he wente so all for somer lyghte . . .
>
> His cote was checked with patches rede and blewe . . .[44]

Bale himself may be recollecting Skelton's poem, since the excuses for "light apparel" so exactly coincide.

I do not imagine that such "light apparel" was ever standardized into a stage-uniform comparable with the fool's motley coat. A grotesque combination of the flashy and the shabby was evidently aimed at: the effect evoked by Hamlet's abuse of Claudius as a "vice of Kings" and "a King of shreds and patches."

CHAPTER IV

CHANGES OF COSTUME

I HAVE suggested that the costumes in Tudor interludes were significant of their wearers. Before a character opened his mouth, his dress spoke for or against him; his speech of introduction served merely to confirm the impression that his clothes had already made. The importance of costume does not, however, end there. Frequently it is by changing the characters' costume that the author impresses his moral meaning on the audience. It was a common phrase that one actor played many parts, and that he changed his stage-personality with his dress. And since so many of the moral interludes are concerned with changes of heart (either falls to wickedness or conversions to virtue) it is appropriate that changes of dress should signify them; for the reformed character has become, theologically speaking, a new man. Besides these complete changes of dress, there are sometimes symbolic alterations to a character's appearance (usually performed by another character in full view of the audience), and with these minor alterations it is best to begin.

A convenient starting-point is found in Bale's *Three Laws*, where the apparelling of the evil characters in garments suggestive of the Roman Church has already been mentioned. Infidelity and his associates have as their purpose the corruption of the three Laws of the play, of which the full title is *A Comedy concernynge thre lawes, of nature, Moses, & Christ, corrupted by the Sodomytes, Pharysees, and Papystes*. All Bale's plays are to some extent dramatizations of ideas already expressed by Tyndale. Tyndale had written, in 1528, "There is difference in the names betwene a Pope, a Cardinall, a bishop, and so forth, and to say a Scribe, a Pharisey, a seniour, and so forth: but the thyng is all one";[1] and the title and theme of *Three Laws* are based on Tyndale's work *An exposition vpon the V. VI. VII. chapters of Mathew, which three chapters are the keye and the dore of the scripture, and the restoring agayne of Moses law corrupte by the Scribes and Pharises. And the exposition is the restoring agayne of Christes lawe corrupte by the Papistes.*[2] In Bale's play, each of the laws appears in turn, to be maltreated by the Roman vices. These latter infect Nature's Law with leprosy, make Moses' Law lame and blind, and either bury or burn Christ's Law. At last a very Lutheran Deus Pater intervenes, "Bannyshynge the sectes, of Babylonicall poperye," and restoring the Laws to their original purity. Of these three episodes the first is Bale's invention, and with savage vivacity he retails hideous scandals of monastic loose-living. The other two, however, are suggested wholly by Tyndale's works. The restoring of Moses' Law from blindness has its counterpart in Tyndale when Christ "plucketh away from the face of Moses, the vaile which the Scribes and Phareises had spred thereon, that no man might perceaue the brightnes of his countenance":[3] this phrase is a Protestant application of II Corinthians iii, and reappears in *Three Laws* as

> On the face of Moyses,
> A vayle they haue cast doughtles.
> The lyght of the lawe to hyde.

The confusion in *Three Laws* over the fate of Christ's Law, who is at one point to be burned ("Burne hym to ashes") and at another to be buried ("Whan ye haue hym in hys graue / Stampe hym downe . . .") results from combining two ideas of Tyndale, who, like Bale, is evidently seeing as mutually symbolic the bodily death and burial of Christ and the burning of Protestant translations of the New Testament. "Rochester and his holy brethren haue burnt Christes Testament: an euident signe verely that they woulde haue burnt Christ him selfe also if they had had him," Tyndale writes; and again "As the olde hypocrites when they had slayne Christ, set pollaxes to keep him in his sepulchre that he should not rise againe: euen so haue our hypocrites buried the testament."[4] Bale elaborates the second of these ideas by adding that the four sentries at the sepulchre of Christ's Law are to be ambitious prelates, covetous lawyers, ignorant lords and wicked judges, who profit from the people's blindness: "These wyll kepe hym downe, and rappe hym on the scull."

Probably the leprosy of Nature's law was indicated by the painted spots which also symbolize corruption in *The Whore of Babylon* and two other plays shortly to be discussed (*Apius and*

Virginia and *Three Ladies of London*).[5] A veil is put over the face of Moses's Law, and this may be either a real veil or, more probably, a blindfolding bandage, as is indicated by the line "Thus a blynde crypple, I wander here alone."[6] Both these transformations take place off the stage, but the cruel handling of Christ's Law begins in full view of the audience, when False Doctrine cries "Laye handes vpon hym, & depryue hym of thys aparell," and the direction is "*Hic veste spoliatum. sordidioribus induunt*," after which Christ's Law is taken out to be burned to ashes.

The interest of the play's relation to Tyndale's writings is that Bale can be seen turning metaphor and simile into dramatic allegory by his use of costume-changes, and amplifying Tyndale's rhetorical hints by means of invented detail calculated to make a powerful effect on an audience. The fact that the disfigurement of Christ's Law is more dramatic than that of the other Laws (because it takes place on stage) is deliberate. It is not only the third and last of a series of parallel incidents, but is also, in its insistence on a vernacular Bible, the point on which Bale is campaigning most fiercely in this play.

The relationship between imagery (especially of the traditional and proverbial kind) and stage-symbolism does not, of course, begin with Bale; it is obviously a natural relationship of great antiquity, and it is probable that a good deal of mutual influence between the popular sermon and the moral play could be traced. *Piers Plowman* continually employs this half-metaphorical, half-allegorical method. The transformation of the Soul and her three powers Mind, Will, and Understanding, in *Wisdom* (about 1460) was perhaps suggested by a sermon. Corrupted by Lucifer, Mind becomes Maintenance (the use of power to pervert justice), and leads red-bearded dancers wearing rampant lions on their crests and carrying warders; Understanding becomes Perjury and leads dancers in jurors' gowns and hoods and caps of maintenance; and Will, now Lechery, leads female "gallants" and "Matrones" (perhaps bawds). The Soul herself has also suffered a change and now enters with a "horrybyll mantyll" from beneath which run demons. On repentance, all are restored to their original appearance, the Soul dressed in white and the three Powers in cloth of gold.

The Tide tarrieth No Man makes a visual moral point by dressing Christianity in the whole armour of God as recommended by St Paul (Ephesians, vi). "Christianity must enter with a sword, with a title of pollicy, but on the other syde of the tytle, must be written gods word, also a shield, wheron must be written riches, but on the other syde of the Shield must be Fayth." Only the worldly titles (or labels) are visible to the spectators, and Christianity's speech expresses how he is "deformed" by the greed of those who are Christians only in name. Faithful Few, who represents the real Christians, enters and turns the titles; but now there appears the wicked merchant Greediness, who is unmoved when Faithful Few reproaches him for having given Christianity not "his righteous Armour" but "the Armour of Sathan," and retorts:

But geue me riches, take you Gods word and fayth,
And see which of vs shall haue the better gayne.
CHRISTIAN.: Now Faithfull few, you here what he sayth,
Therefore to turne the tytles I must be fayne.

It is only at the end of the play, when Greediness is dead in despair and Corage the vice has been hanged, that Faithful Few is able to turn the titles once more.

Before discussing complete changes of costume, it is convenient to mention other plays in which minor alterations are made to the appearance of a character. The (masculine) Conscience of the wicked judge Apius in *Apius and Virginia*, who enters as soon as Apius has decided to ravish Virginia, complains:

I spotted am by wilfull will,
By lawles loue and luste;

the stage direction merely describes Conscience as holding a lamp, but this speech implies visible spots and offers an explanation of them. In *Three Ladies of London*, when Love and Conscience can get no living in a wicked London, their prosperous sister Lucre persuades Conscience to become her bawd for money. Sending her servant Usury home for the money, Lucre secretly bids him also fetch "the boxe of abhomination," which is "painted with diuers colours and is prettie to the show" (there is the usual sinister symbolism of motley here). His reappearance is marked with the direction "Enter Vserie with a paynted boxe of incke in hys hand"; and while Conscience is counting the money paid her by Lucre, "Here let Lucar open the boxe and dip her finger in it, and spotte Conscience face, saying as followeth:"

Hould here my sweete, and [tell] them ouer to see if any want,
The more I doe behold this face, the more my minde doth vaunt:
This face is of fauour, these cheekes are reddy and white,
These lips are cherry red, and full of deepe delight.
Quicke rowling eyes, her temples hygh, and forhead white as snowe,
Her eye-browes seemely set in frame, with dimpled chinne below:

As she enumerates Conscience's beauties, she touches each in turn with an inky finger; the degradation of Conscience is emphasized by drawing the audience's attention to (for instance) a forehead white as snow and immediately spotting it with ink. The fact that Lucre's action is in itself a light-hearted practical joke (commonly played, one supposes, by children) brings out by contrast the sinister moral of the incident.

Characters in sickness tie a kerchief about their head or face, like Caius Ligarius when he visits Brutus in *Julius Caesar*. Brutus cries:

O what a time haue you chose out braue Caius,
To weare a Kerchiefe? Would you were not sicke.

and Ligarius, learning that the conspirators have a noble object in view, makes his recovery dramatic and spectacular by pulling off the kerchief:

By all the Gods that Romans bow before,
I heere discard my sicknesse.

The significance of this kerchief was traditional. In the Marian interlude *Wealth and Health*, when Health, Wealth, and Liberty (who collectively represent the nation's prosperity) have been injured by the evil Shrewd Wit and Ill Will (the Protestant extortioners) "Helth commeth in with a kercher on his head" lamenting that he is infected both in body and in soul. A contemporary German print (Plate IV) shows Krankheit (Sickness) with his face and head bound up in this kerchief, and carrying also a crutch and the bottle used for the inspection of urine in diagnosis. This familiar symbolism is burlesqued in *Fair Em, the Miller's Daughter of Manchester* (about 1594), where the clownish servant Trotter uses it to acquaint Em with his love for her:

Enter Em and Trotter the Millers man with a kerchife on his head, and an Vrinall in his hand.

EM: *Trotter* where haue you bene?
TROTTER: Where haue I beene? Why, what signifies this?

EM: A kerchiefe, doth it not?
TROTTER: What call you this I praye?
EM: I saie it is an Vrinall.
TROTTER: Then this is mystically to giue you to vnderstand I haue beene at the Phismicaries house.[7]

We come now to complete changes of costume, which figure so commonly in the interludes that their various purposes and interpretations must be discussed individually. As has been said in discussing *Three Laws* and *The Tide tarrieth No Man*, the costume-symbolism is fundamentally connected with imagery. Sometimes a momentary use of costume, itself almost as fleeting as an image, occurs. At the beginning of *Three Lords and Three Ladies of London*, for instance, the ladies Love, Conscience, and Lucre enter in rags lamenting their sins committed in the previous play where they appeared. Offering to give them better clothing, "Vsurie takes Frauds cloak, & casts it on Conscience"; the gift is of course instantly repudiated, but an opportunity is provided for Simplicity to observe "Vsury couers Conscience with Frauds cloake verie cunningly."

There is no fundamental connexion between this use of costume and the "disguisings" so popular at Henry VIII's court; the term "disguising" in itself means no more than the "dressing up" of the participants in masquers' costumes. But an incident when "sodeinly the men cast of their large gounes, and then their vnder apparell was seen" hints at the spectacular effect which also accompanies the removal of a disguise (in the modern sense of the word) in the interludes;[8] and the unmasking of the dancers —the frequent climax of the court disguising—suggests the dramatic effect of discovery.[9] The use of costume as an instrument of the plot was dictated not only by allegory and decorum, which demand a change of costume to represent or correspond with a change of character or of circumstances, but also by dramatic and theatrical interest, which call for significant action and spectacle.

Repentance and regeneration, which is a principal theme of most early moral interludes, is often accompanied by a change to a more sober costume. When Death accosts Everyman—

> Euery man stande styll whyder arte thou goynge
> Thus gayly? hast thou thy maker forgete?—

the word "gayly" betrays Everyman's worldly gaiety of dress, which Death exposes and condemns. Later, Everyman repents and accuses his body of vanity: "Also thou delytest to go gay and fresshe." When all those he trusted have refused to accompany him on his last journey, Everyman sinks further and further into despair, but is at length brought by Knowledge to Confession, who presents him with a scourge. In scourging his body, Everyman surely removes his gay cloak; and instead of resuming it he is given a new garment by Knowledge:

KNOWLEGE: Be no more sad but euer reioyce
God seeth thy lyuynge in his trone aboue
Put on this garment to thy behoue
Whiche is wette with your teres
Or elles before god you may it mysse
Whan ye to your iourneys ende come shall.
EUERY MAN: Gentyll knowlege what do ye it call?
KNOWLEGE: It is a garmente of sorowe
Fro payne it wyll you borowe
Contrycyon it is
That getteth forgyuenes
He pleasyth god passynge well.
GOOD DEDES: Euery man wyll you were it for your hele?
EUERY MAN: Now blessyd be Iesu maryes sone
For now haue I on true contrycyon.

Perhaps this garment was the white sheet worn by public penitents, as by the hero of *Impatient Poverty*, and by the Duchess of Gloucester in *2 Henry VI*. Alternatively it might be made of sackcloth, such as is suggested in *The Duchess of Malfi*, when Bosola urges Ferdinand not to drive the Duchess to despair, but instead to

Send her a penitentiall garment, to put on,
Next to her delicate skinne, and furnish her
With beades, and prayer bookes.

It was certainly symbolic of contrition; and if it was white it would also serve convincingly to represent Everyman's shroud when he at last descends into his grave.[10]

Everyman takes place throughout on the spiritual plane, and nearly all the action appears to be within the repentant sinner's soul. It thus differs from *Hickscorner* and *Youth*, in which the multitude of racy topical allusions (the scene is the London of Newgate and the stews) suggest not a conflict in the human soul between good and evil forces, but rather a conflict between good men and sinners whom they finally convert. At the end of *Hick-scorner*, one of the disreputables, Freewill, agrees to "forsake all this worlde wylfully here," to wait on Perseverance and to be God's servant day and night; he retains his name and is rewarded by Perseverance and Contemplation with "a newe garment." When his companion Imagination enters and sees him in it he at first cries scornfully "What felawe is this that in this cote is fyled?", but repents in his turn and also qualifies for "a better clothyng," taking the new name of Good Remembrance. The play gives no account of these new clothes, but a parallel incident in *Youth* may perhaps throw light on them. Youth forsakes the ruffianly debauchee Riot and his own dissolute life, takes the name of Good Contrition, and is given by Charity

> a newe araye
> For to walke by the waye
> Your prayer for to saye.

To this Humility adds:

> Here be bedes for your deuocyon
> And kepe you from all temptacyon
> Let not vyce deuoure
> Whan ye se mysdoing men
> Good counsell geue them
> And teach them to amende.

The repentant Youth, equipped with a rosary and a new garment, praying and converting the wicked as he travels, may have become an itinerant preacher (perhaps a friar like Conscience in *Mundus et Infans*); the possibility is given some support by the fact that in *Hickscorner* the regenerate Freewill takes an active part in converting Imagination. On the other hand, when William Copland reprinted *Youth* in or about 1562, and thought fit to change Humility's gift from beads to books, he let the "newe araye" stand; and (unless he had overlooked it) this suggests that there was nothing offensive to Protestants in the new garment, whatever it was.[11] Of course, Youth could have become a Protestant minister in a staged version of Copland's text. I think, however, that the repentance of the dissolute is hardly enough to qualify them for holy orders, and that a garment symbolizing repentance by its whiteness is the most likely and the most satisfactory solution to this problem.

The interesting point remains that in no plays of Edward VI's reign or later is a change of garments introduced merely as a mark of repentance, though in *Impatient Poverty* it represents the restoration of a repentant sinner to his material prosperity. *Lusty Juventus*, which in spite of its extreme Protestantism has much in common with the earlier *Youth*, ends with Good Counsel rebuking the hero for his cut and jagged clothes but offering him nothing new to wear when he repents. The structure of this interlude, however, may be responsible for its use of costume. Juventus has been reclaimed once already, in the play's first episode, and has received doctrinal instruction from Good Counsel and Knowledge. They make no mention of his depraved costume. The insecure moral position of Juventus is brought out by the fact that in the central episode, where he is tempted into backsliding by Hypocrisy, Fellowship, and Abominable Living, he carries a Bible but must also be still wearing the clothes which earn his final rebuke and which are appropriate to his embracing of Abominable Living the harlot.[12] There is no room allowed at the end for a change of dress, since the concluding prayer immediately follows his second and final repentance.

In *New Custom*, another Protestant play, new garments are actually refused to a repentant evildoer. This is the old Popish priest Perverse Doctrine, who asks for new garments when his adversaries New Custom and Light of the Gospel have persuaded him that his own are not authorized by the Church's primitive constitution; New Custom himself is dressed as a Genevan minister

> With a gathered frocke, a powlde head, and a broad hatte,
> An vnshaued bearde, a pale face . . .

and (according to Perverse Doctrine in the opening scene, where he is a trustworthy witness) inveighs against the square caps and white surplices of priests as superstitious trifles. But at the end of the play he emphatically states that, since the wearing of vestments is "a matter indifferent," consequently:

> hee who puttes his religion in wearing the thing:
> Or thinkes him self more holly for the contrarie doing:
> Shall proue but a foole, of whateuer condition
> Hee bee, for sure that is but meere superstition:

and in conclusion he bids Perverse (now Sincere) Doctrine

vse your apparell, as is comely, and decent,
And not against Scripture any where in my iudgement.

It is very obvious that New Custom's attitude towards the garments of the clergy is self-contradictory, especially since he has himself abandoned the vestments which he now allows Sincere Doctrine to retain, and since these vestments have been specifically recommended to Perverse Doctrine by Hypocrisy.[13] This fact is the more curious in that clerical dress is one of the play's principal topics. It has been suggested that more than one author had a hand in the interlude.[14] Certainly it is said that New Custom "hath not been in the Realme very many yeares," which hardly tallies with the title-page's heavy insistence that the play is one "deuised of late, and for diuerse causes nowe set forth, neuer before this tyme [1573] imprinted," or with the inclusion of material which was not available before the 1570 edition of Foxe's *Actes and Monuments*.[15] Yet there is no apparent difference in style between the different parts of the play.[16] A purposeful reviser, moreover, might be expected to purge the argument of inconsistencies. I think *New Custom* was written by a Protestant who was himself in sympathy with the Genevans but who was willing to compromise with the more traditionally-minded clergy in order to form a solid front against Rome. Controversy about vestments had endangered the unity of Elizabeth's church, particularly in 1563; and the excommunication of Elizabeth in 1570 made unity most necessary at that time.

Degeneration, as well as regeneration, could be effectively shown by means of costume, where the effects of material self-indulgence and vanity were easy to suggest. The first movement towards this is seen in those early plays in which the hero is clothed by the World. In *The Castle of Perseverance*, Mundus gives Humanum Genus rich clothing which causes his temporary over-confidence but is not proof against the spear of Penitence.[17] Several visits to Mundus are made in *Mundus et Infans*, and each time the hero receives garments appropriate to his increasing maturity. When, as Manhood, he is "in robes ryall ryght of good hewe," he is instructed by Conscience, who persuades him to desert the Deadly Sins, but does not object to his clothing:

MANHODE: But yet I praye the syr tell me
May I not go arayde honestly?

CONSCYENCE: Yes manhode hardely
In all maner of degre.

Evidently Manhood is now in a state of wordly prosperity which is good or evil according to the life he proposes to lead. When he is tempted by Folly, and falls, nothing is made of this in terms of costume. In Medwall's *Nature*, however, a gradual degeneration is presented. The play opens like *The Castle of Perseverance*; at Nature's command, Man goes to the World, who is astonished to find him naked, says that climate and custom require more than the "garment of innocencye," and clothes him in a gown, cap, and girdle.[18] There is no indication that Man has as yet become worldly in any bad sense; Reason and Innocency both offer advice, but this is merely advice to avoid sin in his now responsible position, not to abandon a sin already committed. It is only in now ordering him to associate with merry companions, "be they neuer so vycyouse or abhominable," and in replacing Innocency with Worldly Affection, that the World becomes sinister. Worldly Affection assists Sensuality in gaining Man's ear, and sends in Pride, who devises for Man a "gallant" costume more extravagant than his own. It consists of a gown freely adorned with broad lace, an open-backed and sleeveless doublet, a white silk shirt, velvet striped breeches, and multi-coloured hose. During Man's first lapse and temporary repentance this dress is being made, and he is not seen in it until the second part of the play, when it makes him appear deeper in sin than he was before. There is no sign that when he repents in his old age he has changed into anything more sober, and perhaps he is still incongruously wearing the "gallant" costume when he receives advice from the virtues (if this is so, "Vse none aray that staryng ys to syght" carries particular force), and changes it only off-stage during his visit to Repentance before his final appearance. Whether or not this is so, the point of the play is clearly that there are degrees of worldliness, the first equivalent to experience and the second to sin.

Mankind also shows the hero's degeneration, this time by the fate of his side-gown, a dress of unusual gravity for a tiller of the soil such as Mankind is in this play, and therefore to be understood as a symbol of his moral respectability. The worldly buffoons, Newguise, Nowadays, and Nought, who are his tempters, suggest that it might fetch money if sold. Newguise takes it out and returns with a trifling jacket, which Nought still further shortens. Mankind is thus shown losing his reputation because of the company he keeps.

In contrast, the Worldly Man's apparel in Wager's *Enough is as good as a Feast* grows rich while his soul grows mean. In this Elizabethan interlude, where the moral put forward is social, extreme prosperity becomes a sign of guilt. The hero is an ambitious worldly climber, and his gradual attainment (or apparent attainment) of his ambitions must be visually represented. He first enters "stout and frolike," having great wealth but aspiring to more. Converted by Heavenly Man, he has given away twenty pounds when he next appears, "in a straunge attire." It is regrettable that this direction is not more precise; all that can be said with certainty is that he has changed his costume, but the fact that he is now consorting with "poorly arayed" Enough suggests that his costume is now less grandiose than formerly. Perhaps he had originally worn the furred gown traditionally associated with the usurer, and now abandons this sign of his former life.[19] Guided by Covetous, he reverts to extortion, and his moment of triumph is marked by his entrance "all braue." But the author has prepared retribution for him and he sickens, dies, and is carried off to Hell in all his finery.

In the course of another of William Wager's plays, *The longer thou livest the more Fool thou art*, the ridiculous and evil hero Moros is elevated to authority by Fortune ("A popish foole will I place in a wisemans seate") and enters "gaily disguised and with a foolish beard." He resolves to persecute Protestants, but is felled by God's Judgment and despoiled of his robes, chain and staff of office by Confusion, who gives him instead a fool's coat and carries him off to Hell. In this scene costume is used to point out how the value capriciously set on Moros by Fortune differs from his real worthlessness which is known to God.

The costume of the fool is again used dramatically in *Ane Satyre of the Thrie Estaitis* to expose the wicked clergy. Here the bishop Spiritualitie and his subordinates the Abbot and the Parson have fettered Veritie and banishèd Chastitie, have robbed Pauper and John the Common Weill, and have been exposed by Divyne Correction as unfit to hold spiritual office. The officers of the law disrobe them and invest three worthier clerks in their place. Then the Merchant addresses the degraded clergy:

We mervell of yow paintit sepulturis,
That was sa bauld for to accept sic cuiris,
With glorious habite rydand vpon your Muillis.
Now men may se ye ar bot verie fuillis.

SPIRITUALITIE: We say the Kings war greiter fuillis nor we,
That vs promovit to sa greit dignitie.

ABBOT: Thair is ane thowsand in the kirk but doubt,
Sic fuillis as we gif thay war weill socht out.

Rejected as fools even by Sensuality and Covetyce, they trudge off to make their living as best they can.[20]

A third play in which the fool's coat provides a moral comment is Redford's *Wit and Science*, which continually and subtly exploits the meaning of costume. The hero evidently begins his quest in a young scholar's gown, with "garmentes of science" on his back; but when he grows over-fond of Honest Recreation and insists on dancing with her he throws off the gown, forsaking Science thereby:

HONESTE RECREACYON: then for a whyle
ye must excyle
this garment cumbryng.

WYT: In deede as ye say
this cumbrus aray
woold make wyt slumbryng

HONEST RECREACION: yt is gay geere
of science cleere
yt seemth her aray.

WYT: whose ever it were
yt lythe now there.

HONEST RECREACION: go to my men play.

After the galliard he sinks into the arms of Idleness, who blackens his face, perhaps to show how obscured his wit has become.[21] She calls in the fool Ingnorance (*sic*) and puts his coat on Wit, giving him in exchange the gown which lies near the sleeper. But though Wit continues to sleep peacefully in the fool's coat, Ingnorance is unable to keep the gown from slipping off his back, and Idleness explains that this is because it is Science's garment and therefore inappropriate wear for fools. When Wit awakens he forgets his follies and complacently resumes his courtship of Science, whose scorn and indignation surprise him until he looks in his glass. He is beaten by Shame, to whom Reason gets rid of the fool's coat, and is led out by Reason to receive the "new aparell" which his repentance has earned, probably his original gown again. When he has vanquished Tediousness, Science sends him a "gowne of knoledge" in which he is invested for the betrothal ceremony: this may well be a master's gown.

The episode of the dance finds a parallel in *Impatient Poverty*. Here the hero is raised by Peace from his original poor estate. His name is changed from Poverty to Prosperity, and his "bare" and "poore" array to a new "vesture," unspecified but presumably including a rich cloak. He is now tempted by Envy and Misrule to gaming and fornication, but before the three leave the place Envy cries

> Of wyth this lewde araye
> It becommeth you nought by this daye,

and Prosperity replies

> By my trouth euen as ye saye
> Ye marye nowe am I well apayde
> Me thynketh I am properly araide:

and, Misrule suggesting that they dance a French round, he shouts

> And thou shalt se me bounce aboue the grounde.

The audience would be quick to appreciate the dramatic irony of these remarks: Prosperity means merely that without his upper garment he enjoys more freedom to revel and dance, but the spectators perceive that the decadent reveller is very properly stripping himself out of the prosperity which his conduct forfeits. When he next appears he has lost his money at dice, and is once more reduced to Poverty, in name, condition and dress: "And then entreth prosperite poorely" indicates a meaner dress than he has yet worn, perhaps the beggar's rags. He does penance in a white sheet—though this is a token not so much of his repentance as of his persecution by a wicked Summoner whom he cannot afford to bribe—and, when he is genuinely contrite, is rewarded by Peace with full restoration to the name and condition of Prosperity: "Wyth thys vesture I shal the renewe."

The costumes are frequently used, as here, to show changes in material prosperity. Sometimes the change is a literal reduction to beggary when prodigals lose their money (*The Disobedient Child*, *The Nice Wanton*, *Like will to Like*); sometimes, as when Money escapes from Prodigality in tattered clothing (*Liberality and Prodigality*), it is wholly allegorical. In *Three Ladies of London*, when Lucre raises the rent of houses in London so that Love and Conscience are obliged to pawn their gowns in order to pay for living there, the literal truth that poor tenants must raise the rent by pledging their clothes is used to signify that London is so corrupt that neighbourly love and personal conscience are almost driven out and are greatly decayed.

Plays which point a political moral usually end with a costume-change, in which the national prosperity is restored after thoughtless or selfish abuse. Skelton's *Magnificence*, the earliest of these Tudor plays on political themes, is also the widest in moral scope, since Magnificence is not only the extravagant and guileless ruler who has ruined himself but also any human soul struck down by adversity; and when Adversity appears and "Magnyfycence is beten downe and spoylyd from all his goodys and rayment," given rags by Poverty, and tempted by Despair, the practical political moral becomes temporarily submerged beneath the spiritual one, though it is resumed when Magnificence is restored to his crown and wealth, a new "abylyment," and "Ioy and Ryalte." The later plays, though their general political theme is akin to that of Skelton's, treat this costume-change purely in terms of material rehabilitation. At the end of Lyndsay's *Satyre of the Thrie Estaitis* John the Common Weill exchanges his rags for new robes of "Sating, Damais, or of the Velvot fyne." The heroine of *Respublica*, on whom Avarice and his fellows have preyed under the pretence of offering help, is taken out by Verity and the other virtues "to be Newe appareled otherwyse then thus," and when she returns Avarice wryly congratulates her on being "so gorgeously decked and so gaye"; the restoration of People in the same play is still more obviously a material one, since he explains that he now has a new coat because for the first time in many years he can afford one.

The last important purpose of a character's change of costume is to assume a disguise. The pretence of vices to be virtues is a theme almost universal in the interludes, and in allegorical literature in general (the disguises of Archimago and Duessa in Spenser immediately come to mind).[22] Apart from the dramatic interest attaching to disguise, excellent opportunities must have been provided for stage business. The audience of *Respublica*, for example, would be diverted by the vigilance of Avarice and his friends to hide their identities and their loot under their gowns, and by the struggles attending the final stripping-off of these disguises.

Originally it seems to have been the devil who disguised himself. In the *Ludus Coventriae* cycle he is dressed as a gallant. This is not, in the strict dramatic sense of the word, a disguise, since he reveals his name at once, and the purpose of the costume is to show the devilish nature of pride. But his speech, in its use of euphemisms for the Deadly Sins ("Ye xal kalle pryde oneste and naturall kind lechory / And covetyse wysdam . . ."),[23] looks forward to those Tudor interludes in which the sins are introduced to their dupes under false names, as in *The longer thou livest the more Fool thou art*, where Idleness is Pastime, Incontinence Pleasure, Wrath Manhood, Impiety Philosophy, Cruelty Prudence, and Ignorance Antiquity. The devil's disguise as a gallant is to put to a dramatic use in *Wisdom*, where Lucifer does thereby conceal his real identity from the Mind, Will, and Understanding of the Soul. In Bale's *The Temptation of Our Lord*, Satan's disguise as a hermit has nominally the same dramatic purpose of concealing his diabolical identity while he tempts Christ; but the use which Bale makes of the disguising is rather polemical than dramatic, for when Christ exposes the devil beneath the religious habit, Bale is discrediting the feigned contemplative life. The satirical effect is comparable with that of the friar's garb clothing Mephistophilis in *Doctor Faustus*: "That holy shape becomes a diuell best."

In *King John*, Bale refines this technique until it becomes highly dramatic, as well as a sharp instrument of satire. Thus Sedition, having effectively revealed himself to the king as a "lewde person" through his scurrilous remarks, hurries away at Nobility's approach to change his apparel. ("I wold not be sene, as I am, for fortye pence.") He knows that he can best pervert Nobility from loyalty to the king by putting on a garb of religion, and it is as Stephen Langton that he first appears in Nobility's sight.

The scene in which he assumes the personality and dress of the archbishop is worth attention. Sedition, Usurped Power, and Private Wealth are all clothed like rogues until they change their dress and return as Stephen Langton, the Pope, and Cardinal Pandulphus. This change of costume takes place during a monologue supplied by Dissimulation, who is already dressed as a monk in a many-coloured habit. It is to be noted, however, that they are becoming these individuals neither as a mere disguise nor for the first time. Private Wealth has already explained that Usurped Power is really the Pope also, in spite of his discreditable appearance. This is not disguise, but satirical allegory, directed at the Pope. Similarly, Sedition has a real personal existence as Stephen Langton: this is clear when Usurped Power, who is complaining to the others that King John is "alwayes contrary," says in illustration:

> I made this fellow here, the arche bysshope of canterbery
> & he [*i.e.* John] wyll agree, therto in no condycyon.
> PRIVAT WELTH: than hathe he knowlege, that his name ys sedycyon?
> DYSSYMULACYON: dowtles he hathe so, & that drownnyth his opynyon.
> VSURPID POWER: why do ye not saye, his name ys stevyn langton?
> DYSSYMULACYON: tushe we haue done so, but that helpyth not the mater.
> the bysshope of norwyche, for that cawse dothe hym flater.
> VSURPID POWER: styke thow to yt fast, we haue onys admytted the.
> SEDYCYON: I wyll not one Iote, from my admyssyon fle.
> the best of them all, shall know that I am he.[24]

This dialogue precedes the change of costumes, and its purpose is to show that Sedition and his fellows can exist in many shapes, and also that the seditious archbishop is sedition personified.

Lewis Wager's *Mary Magdalene* owes a good deal in its spirit and methods to the plays of Bale. Here the vice is Infidelity, who, like Sedition, can exist in more shapes than one, and whose boast is:

> For euery day I haue a garment to weare,
> Accordyng to my worke and operation.

His purpose is to corrupt Mary, and he puts on "a gowne & a cap" in order to impress her; later, to confront Christ at Simon's house, he requires a cap and robe of a pharisee:

> About the which the preceptes of the testament
> Must be written in order one by one.

Just as Bale presents Stephen Langton as the embodiment of Sedition, so Lewis Wager presents a Pharisee as the embodiment of Infidelity.

The gown and cap in which Infidelity deceives Mary seems to be the secular costume of a man of wealth and dignity. This costume is required also in William Wager's *Enough is as good as a Feast*, where the vice Covetous learns that his intended dupe Worldly Man has left his avaricious life. Covetous exclaims

> Body of me *Precipitation*, fetch me my gown:
> My Cap, and my Chain, I wil to the Town.

When Covetous has disguised himself there is some derisive banter between him and his fellows, but Inconsideration's remark

> It is trim indeed, by the masse in that Gown:
> Me thinks you be worthy to be Mayor of a town

confirms that this is the costume of a wealthy burgess, however disreputable the wearer himself may be.

An assumed dress, like an assumed name, is a means whereby evil characters purchase credit. The disguisings of rogues in *Respublica* and *Ane Satyre of the Thrie Estaitis* are of special interest and are discussed separately. It is not to be supposed, however, that the change of name necessarily involves a change of dress. Thus in *Impatient Poverty* Envy calls himself Charity in order to deceive Conscience and pervert Prosperity; but since neither has seen him during his earlier appearances under his true name, there is no need for him to disguise himself. W. J. Lawrence, thinking that a disguise was worn, fears that the audience would confuse disguise with the doubling of parts (Envy doubles with the Summoner, and the eight parts are played by four actors);[25] but in fact the author has been careful to avoid such confusion by making Envy retain his original dress, which may well be shabby, since the proud Prosperity disdains the supposed Charity as a "pore haskarde," or contemptible fellow. When a character does disguise himself, it is usual for him to do so on stage, the act being not only theatrically interesting but also morally significant: for it shows, firstly, that he retains his own nature, and secondly, that he is therefore a dissembler.

Disguise is not always morally significant, even in moral interludes. Sometimes it is merely comic. In *The Marriage of Wit and Wisdom* the vice Idleness exists mainly to provide episodic farce, and dresses successively as a foreign doctor, a lame rat-catcher, and a priest; only in the last of these disguises, with the satirical invitation "Thay that list not to worke let them follow me," does he attain even a casual moral importance.[26] Similarly, in *Three Lords and Three Ladies of London*, Fraud and Dissimulation are caught up in the cheerful whirl of the marriage festivities at the end, and amusingly appear disguised as extras in blue gowns with red caps and red sleeves. *The Pedlar's Prophecy* ends with a pleasant scene full of mild irony, in which a Justice (who is trying to track down the Pedlar, judging him a seditious discloser of abuses best kept secret) meets with the Pedlar himself in his disguise as a priest and learns from him that the Pedlar is "a litle man sir, euen of my stature."

The disguising of the vices in *Respublica* requires individual consideration. This interlude celebrates Mary's accession, and condemns the changes in church and state introduced in the two previous reigns as the combined work of Avarice, Insolence, Oppression, and Adulation. In the prefatory list of characters Avarice is described as "the vice of the plaie" and his three confederates as "gallants" (they are called collectively "vices" in the text). The deceits of four impostors had already been the subject of Skelton's *Magnificence*, and the prologue to *Respublica* recalls the names of Cloaked Collusion, Counterfeit Countenance, and Courtly Abusion from Skelton's play:

> But thoughe these vices by cloked collusyon
> And by counterfaicte Names, hidden theire abusion
> Do Reigne for a while to common weales preiudice
> Pervertinge all right and all ordre of true Iustice
> Yet tyme trieth all and tyme bringeth truth to lyght
> That wronge maye not ever still reigne in place of right.

To deceive and defraud Respublica, all four take false names and conceal their garments under cloaks, robes, or gowns. This is obviously necessary for Avarice, who must hide the purses hanging at his back.[27] The others, however, are not equipped with purses (this can safely be assumed, as there is no reference to them, while Avarice's are important), and the reason for their disguise is less clear—unless it is only in their disguises that they are "gallants" (or, as People describes them, "a zorte of courtnalls" or courtiers).[28] This is perhaps hinted when Oppression asks Avarice why they too must disguise themselves, and is satisfied with the reply

> All folke wyll take yowe, if they piepe vnder youre gowne,
> for the veriest catif in Countrey or towne:

which suggests that they are disreputably dressed. At the end of the play, however, when Verity has told Respublica who these rogues really are, she adds "Ye shall see yt proved trewe before your owne face"; and then, after revealing the purses beneath Avarice's cloak, she bids the other "counterfaictes" remove theirs:

> Sirs, doe of your vtmoste robes eche one even heare,
> Now what these are yee see plaine demonstration.
>
> RESPUBLICA: Insolence, Oppression, Adulation.

From this it appears that each can be identified, and by means of what he wears under his cloak; yet the play reveals nothing about their several costumes. Perhaps each has his name written on his breast: for when the cloaks come off, Respublica seems to read them out. If this is so, it explains why the line should consist simply of the three names, with a pause between each and the next. There is precedent for such labelling of characters, in plays as well as in pageants, during the sixteenth century.[29]

CHAPTER V

ACTION

It is my intention, in this final chapter, first to discuss some significant pieces of stage business; and then to suggest, by means of analysing two representative plays, how effective the Tudor interlude could be in performance.

Action, like costume, is often charged with moral weight in the interludes. Sometimes an event is expected and its significance obvious: Wit marries Science and the scholar attains his goal, Falset and Dissait are hanged and society's blemishes are cured. Some important incidents, however, are neither the mainsprings nor the necessary conclusions of the plots, and it is these which now need investigation.

One such incident is the temporary fettering, sometimes in the stocks, of a virtue by the vices. This occurs in *Youth*, *Hickscorner*, and *Ane Satyre of the Thrie Estaitis*.

In *Hickscorner*, the incident is treated realistically and made into a warning against bearing false witness. The criminal rioters Hickscorner, Imagination, and Freewill conspire to accuse Pity of stealing forty pounds from Imagination; the accusation is made, Hickscorner threatening Pity with imprisonment in Newgate, Freewill bringing a pair of gyves for Pity's feet, and Imagination producing a halter with which to bind his hands. Pity exhorts them (and the audience):

> O men let trouth that is the trewe man
> Be your guyder or elles ye be forlore
> Laye no fals wytnes as nye as ye can
> On none for afterwarde ye wyll repent hyt full sore.

He warns them of God's judgment "whan deth with his mace dooth you areest." Freewill's confident reply recalls the rash resolution of the rioters in Chaucer's *Pardoner's Tale*:

> What dethe and he were here he sholde syt by the.
> Trowest thou that he be able to stryue with vs thre?
> Nay nay nay.

In his fetters, Pity moralizes on the wickedness of the worldly. After his soliloquy he is released by Contemplation and Perseverance, who convert Freewill and Imagination when they return.

There is a parallel incident in *Youth*, where (as in *Hickscorner*) the imprisonment of a virtue is the principal piece of physical action. Youth complains to Riot that Charity has rebuked his dissolute life; Riot swears to beat Charity if he returns, adding:

> And he wyl not be ruled with knockes
> We shall set him in the stockes
> To heale his sore shinnes.

He introduces Youth to Pride, and the three are just going to the tavern when Charity reappears and stays them. Riot, threatening him, goes to fetch a pair of fetters:

> I shal fet a payre of rynges
> That shall sit to his shinnes
> And that euen anone.

Like Pity in *Hickscorner*, Charity is not only fettered about the ankles but also bound at the wrists, for Humility says when loosing him:

> Sir I shall vndo the bandes
> From your feete and your handes.

But this imprisonment, unlike that in *Hickscorner*, is not on a trumped-up charge; instead it is wholly symbolic of Charity's powerlessness in a mind where Riot holds sway. This is also the principal significance of the stocks in *Ane Satyre of the Thrie Estaitis*; though they are put to a practical use at the end of the play (to secure malefactors before their hanging), their symbolic use comes earlier, first when Veritie is imprisoned there by the wicked clergy, and later when Chastitie is set beside her, having been expelled by King Humanitie's mistress Sensualitie. As Veritie is imprisoned she is told:

> This nicht ye sall forfair ane pair of stocks,
> And syn the morne be brocht to thoill Iudgment;

and Flatterie replies to her patient:

> Now Lords do as ye list,
> I haue na mair to say,

with the exultant derision of

Sit doun and tak yow rest,
All nicht till it be day.

Other, lost plays may have employed this device, for it seems to have been widespread and not confined to the stage. In a satirical woodcut by the German artist Peter Flettner (1525), Justice has been imprisoned in the stocks by Usury and Tyranny (Plate V; the fact that Flettner's picture was re-engraved as late as 1647 testifies to the continuing life of the tradition), and in 1524 Albrecht Dürer designed a tapestry showing Justice, Truth, and Reason in the stocks.[1] Some Tudor interludes which do not stage the incident refer to it, and to set the virtues in the stocks is often the first method of dealing with them that comes into their opponents' minds. Thus in *Impatient Poverty*, when Poverty has been elevated by Peace to the rank and name of Prosperity, he becomes a decadent and prodigal reveller, associating with Envy and Misrule. As these three are dancing out in search of low pleasures, Peace appears and warns Prosperity, who furiously bids his friends

Go set hym in a payre of stockes
That I hym no more se.

(They do not, however, act on this; instead they threaten Peace and drive him out.) In *New Custom*, too, Ignorance recommends the stocks as the best means of hindering New Custom's preaching:

For hee hath seduced the people by mightie greate flockes.
Bodie of God, it were good to set the knaue in the stockes.
Or elles to whype him for an exaumple to all roges as hee,
How they the aucthors of newe heresies bee.

In *King Darius*, the vice scornfully offers Equity a fetter for his legs.

When Kent is placed in the stocks by Regan and Cornwall in *King Lear*, the incident derives some of its force from this tradition. Kent is certainly a moral spokesman in the play, even in his disguise, and his soliloquy in the stocks is a focal point in the action, like the monologues of Pity and Charity. The devices of the moral interludes are suggested more than once in *King Lear*; there are, for example, Edgar's description of the grotesque devil whom he feigns to have seen tempting Gloucester to despair, and his speeches about the similar temptations which he claims to have suffered as Poor Tom.

Another incident of the London public stage is Tamburlaine's entry in his chariot, to which he harnesses first the kings of Trebizon and Soria, and later those of Natolia and Jerusalem. This may be compared with the triumphant entry of Fortune in *Liberality and Prodigality*: "Enter Fortune in her Chariot drawne with Kings." It has been thought that Tamburlaine's chariot inspired Fortune's.[2] There are, however, good reasons for supposing that *Liberality and Prodigality* was not a new play when it was published in 1602 but an old one brought up to date, and that the king-drawn chariot was not an interpolation. Indeed, the whole significance of Tamburlaine's chariot, as I see it, is that he is usurping Fortune's attributes. He has already made it clear that, far from submitting to Fortune, he dominates even her:

> I hold the Fates bound fast in yron chaines,
> And with my hand turne Fortunes wheel about,
> And sooner shall the Sun fall from his Spheare,
> Than *Tamburlaine* be slaine or ouercome.[3]

Fortune's control over kings, exalting and deposing them by turning her wheel on which they rode, was a commonplace. The author of *Liberality and Prodigality* gave her a king-drawn chariot for several reasons: it can be represented on stage far more easily than Fortune's wheel; it provides Fortune with a method of entrance; and it renders this entrance spectacular after the manner of those mobile pageants which appeared in royal entry processions and frequently employed allegory. The pulling of Lucifera's chariot by the Deadly Sins (each mounted on an appropriate beast) in *The Faerie Queene* illustrates the device admirably, and so do pictorial allegories (Plate XI).

Riding in her chariot, and accompanied by singing attendants—who certainly do not stay outside as has been wrongly suggested[4]—Fortune enters her palace, where she ascends her stately throne. The ceremony of enthronement appears in other interludes. It is implied in the laconic direction which opens Medwall's *Nature*: "Fyrst cometh in Mundus and syttyth downe & sayth nothyng and wyth hym Worldly affeccyon." The World is a king and his seat is a throne; and when Man visits him and is bidden by him "Syt down as ye ar borne to occupye thys place," Man's enthronement is to be taken as meaning that he has inherited the World's pleasures and dangers. Near the end of some plays conspicuous for their severe moral judgments the virtuous characters are given crowns of spiritual felicity when the vicious perish; Virtuous Life, the Christian in *Like will to Like*, and Just, his counterpart in *The Trial of Treasure*, are so rewarded, but the scenes are sternly shorn of pomp, as befits the self-denial of the characters. In the former play, for instance, the "chaire" in which Virtuous Life is enthroned has earlier been occupied by the vice (judging which of two rogues is pre-eminent) and by Hance (a Fleming in a drunken stupor) and cannot therefore have been in any way decorated or distinguished. In *The Trial of Treasure*, Just is not enthroned at all, and is merely presented or invested with his crown.

At times the significance of a procession lies in its order. Lyndsay's Three Estates enter to the parliament "gangand backwart, led be thair vycis," and John the Common Weill explains to King Humanitie that this is the cause of all the nation's ills:

> As for our reverent fathers of Spiritualitie,
> Thay ar led be Covetice and cairles Sensualitie.
> And as ye se Temporalitie hes neid of correctioun,
> Quhilk hes lang tyme bene led be Publick Oppressioun.
> Loe quhair the loun lyis lurkand at his back.
> Get vp, I think to se thy craig gar ane raip crack.
> Loe heir is Falset and Dissait weill I ken,
> Leiders of the Merchants and sillie crafts-men.
> Quhat mervell thocht the Thrie Estaits backwart gang,
> Quhen sic an vyle cumpanie dwels them amang?

Here the backward walking of the Three Estates symbolizes their self-abandonment to their vices and also implies that the realm's affairs go backward (deteriorate) because of this corruption.

In Bale's *King John*, formal action of this kind is used to show how one evil brings in another. Sedition the vice is plotting with Dissimulation to bring about King John's downfall and the supremacy of Rome. To do this they require the help of Private Wealth and Usurped Power. Sedition bids Dissimulation fetch them both, but he objects:

> I can bryng but one, be mary Iesus mother:

to which Sedition replies:

> Bryng thow in the one, & let hym bryng in the other.

Though a stage-direction (afterwards inserted) bids Private Wealth and Usurped Power enter here, they are merely heard chanting outside.[5] Dissimulation goes to fetch Private Wealth, while Sedition explains to the audience that when the dissembling clergy have thereby grown wealthy they claim unauthorized powers, whence sedition flourishes. Dissimulation now leads in Private Wealth, and introduces him to Sedition before sending him out again with the command:

> feche thow in thy felow, as fast as euer thow can.

This he does, and Usurped Power is cordially welcomed. Then Sedition says:

> nay Vsurpid power, thou must go backe ageyne
> for I must also, put the to a lytyll payne.
> VSURPID POWER: why fellaue sedycyon, what wylt thou haue me do?
> SEDYCYON: to bare me on thi backe, & bryng me in also
> that yt maye be sayde, that fyrst dyssymulacyon
> browght In privat welth, to euery cristen nacyon
> & that privat welth, browght In Vsurpid power
> & he sedycyon, In cytye towne & tower
> that sum man may know, the feche of all ower sorte.
> VSURPID POWER: cum on thy wayes than, that thow mayst mak the fort [*i.e.* the fourth].
> DISSYMULACYON: nay vsurped power, we shall bare hym all thre,
> thy selfe he & I, yf ye wyll be rewlyd by me,
> for ther is non of vs, but in hym hath a stroke.
> PRIVAT WELTH: the horson knaue wayeth, & yt were a Croked oke.

Accordingly there is a change of plan, and all three combine to carry Sedition. It is clear, however, that Bale means this tableau to be grotesque as well as symbolic, for Sedition shouts "I wyll beshyte yow all yf ye sett me not downe softe."

This scene from *King John* shows how important is the manner in which a significant action is performed. Other interludes help to form the audience's response to a situation in a similar way. In *The Trial of Treasure*, immediately after Lust has made his pact of fellowship with the vice Inclination (the natural inclination to evil) and his associated sins, formally embracing each of them in turn, he is seized with pain (the stage-direction bids him "bowe to the grounde") and cries out that he is dying:

> Out alas, what a sodaine passion is this,
> I am so taken that I can not stande,

> The crampe, the crampe, hath touched me, ywis,
> I shall die without remedie nowe out of hand.

This looks like immediate divine retribution upon the sinner before his sinful life has been exhibited (the incident is early in the play), but Inclination's next words dispel such a fear; he tells the other vices:

> This crampe doth signifie nothing in effect
> But howe he is bowed by me Inclination,
> None of all your counsels he will nowe reiecte,
> And therefore feare not to make full declaration.

The vices then proceed to instruct Lust, who significantly bargains:

> Leade me Inclination to haue my desire,
> And then at thy request I wyll euer bende & bowe.

He is led by him straightway to Carnal Cogitation, with Inclination explaining as they leave the place "That I go before is but nedefull and iust." There is plenty of such symbolic action in the play. Inclination is literally bridled by Just, and finally shackled also, and the conflict between Just and Lust with which the play opens is presented as an actual wrestling-bout, in which the overthrow of the vicious young gallant by the older plainly-dressed man is like the homely Kent's cudgelling of the decadent Oswald in *King Lear*.[6] The designed effect on the spectators when Inclination explains Lust's cramp is an interesting one: shock and fear are abruptly dispelled, and Lust's dismay becomes in retrospect ridiculous. By such means as this, we are encouraged to observe Lust's progress with contempt; till at the end of the play, when Time hales him off to destruction, the sinner's anguished cry "Whither go I now, to misery or bliss?" (a query to which we all know the answer well enough) provokes ferocious mirth as well as the terror that accompanies this scene of damnation.

*

In this and the preceding chapters I have tried to show something of the principles according to which the Tudor interludes were performed. By way of epilogue and conclusion, I wish now to illustrate these principles by analysing the whole action of two Elizabethan interludes, *Enough is as good as a Feast* (William Wager; 1564?) and *Liberality and Prodigality* (Sebastian Westcott?;

1567?). I have chosen these two plays for several reasons. They are written for performance in different settings: *Enough is as good as a Feast* admirably illustrates the use of an unfurnished acting-space, whereas *Liberality and Prodigality* equally well displays the scenic resources of the court, where the play was acted by boys before the Queen. Statements in the text of *Liberality and Prodigality*, supported by items in the revels accounts, tell us all these things. About *Enough is as good as a Feast*, on the other hand, scarcely anything is known for certain, but it can be safely guessed that it was not written for the court. Though the topic of both plays is the worldly desire for wealth, and the misuse of it, their purposes are entirely different. *Liberality and Prodigality* is an entertainment, an aristocratic pastime; it is by no means a cynical play, but the moral issues which it brushes are treated with an air of well-bred reasonableness as matters on which there can be no disagreement; and though generosity is recommended to the Queen, it is recommended as a virtue which she already practises, so that the moral advice is not at all contrary to the complimentary nature of the play. Wager's interlude, on the other hand, has no time for compliment. It is a serious play, full of argument and exhortation, and the final prayer that the Last Judgment may recognize the audience and the actors as heavenly men is obviously sincere. The moral instruction is not dry and tedious, but is passionate and urgent, related to the daily living and the ultimate fate of the spectators. It may be like a sermon, but it is a vigorous Tudor sermon that it resembles, a sermon preached by such a man as Latimer.

Enough is as good as a Feast.

The prologue is the least attractive part of the play. Wager is far better at writing plays than he is at writing about the playwright's art, and the latinate rhyme-royal stanzas, laboriously invoking the Muses and diffusely stating the virtues and difficulties of eloquence, are sluggish and heavy. When the Worldly Man replaces the Prologue, his speech is full of life and energy, stuffed with the proverbs of worldly wisdom:

> Because I am a man indewed with treasure,
> Therfore a worldly man men doo me call:
> In deed I haue riches and money at my pleasure,
> Yea, and I wil haue more in spight of them all.

> A common saying better is enuy then rueth,
> I had rather they should spite then pitty me:
> For the olde saying now a dayes proueth trueth,
> Naught haue naught set by as dayly we see.
> I wis I am not of the minde as some men are,
> Which look for no more then wil serue necessitie:
> No against a day to come I doo prepare,
> That when age commeth I may liue merily.
> Oh saith one inough is as good as a feast,
> Yea, but who can tel what his end shal be?
> Therfore I count him wurse then a Beast,
> That wil not haue that in respect and see.
> As by mine owne Father an example I may take,
> He was beloued of all men and kept a good house:
> Whilst riches lasted, but when that did slake,
> There was no man that did set by him a Louse.
> And so at such time as he from the world went,
> I mene when he dyed he was not worth a grote:
> And they that all his substance had spent,
> For the value of xij. pence would haue cut his throte.
> But I trowe I wil take heed of such,
> They shall go ere they drink when they come to me:
> It dooth me good to tel the chinks in my hutch,
> More then at the Tauern or ale house to be.

It should be noted that the Worldly Man is not unprovided with arguments. Improvidence can be wicked, as he says. But the audience is invited to see that his logic is false. The possibility that others may treat us selfishly does not justify our selfishness as a precaution. Covetousness is not the only alternative to waste. There is also the suggestion, supported by the final mention of tavern and alehouse, that the Worldly Man's father did not practise true hospitality but "kept a good house" for revellers who spent his substance. Attention is drawn to these false arguments by the obvious greed of the first quatrain, and by the implication in the third that the speaker is the Rich Fool, preparing for a prosperous and self-indulgent old age; the corollary, that before the end of the play his soul will be required of him, is also implied.

The speech is directed at the audience, a public speech like the prologue, though of course in a colloquial style. The Worldly Man is justifying himself, expounding what he presents as a natural and proper way of life. He blandly assumes that he is persuading the hearers to applaud his worldly wisdom—a good device on Wager's part for arousing their opposition, which is maintained by such ironies as "Yea, but who can tel what his end shal be?" (the speaker's thoughts are limited to material welfare; his own spiritual end is far from his mind). These confidences of the self-assured Worldly Man continue during his ensuing debate with the Heavenly Man and Contentation ("Oh, I tel you these are godly walkers"; "Good reasoning betwixt vs now hear you shall"), and the debate is carried on in full knowledge that it is a public one, so that the exhortations of the Heavenly Man are not addressed solely to his opponent but also to the listeners:

> O you ancient men whome God hath furnished with fame,
> Be ye alwaies mindeful to walke in the waies of the Just . . .
>
> Ye poor men and commons walke in your vocation . . .

The conversion of Worldly Man is not gradual, but suddenly occurs when the argument has run its course. It is to be taken as genuine, and his absolute statement

> For I regarde neither treasure, Children nor wife

is paralleled by the action of Bunyan's Christian who leaves his family behind him in the City of Destruction. Wager is not concerned with the psychology of conversion but with the dramatic expression of it. Being totally unexpected, it is effective. (It is usual—in *Youth* and *Hickscorner*, for instance, or in Wager's own *The longer thou livest the more Fool thou art* and *The Trial of Treasure*—for the evildoers to resist the prayers and warnings of the just, whether they are to be at last reclaimed or destroyed.) Worldly Man takes Heavenly Man by the hand in formal alliance and they go out.

Immediately the vices come in singing the praises of their leader Covetous, who enters next with a long nonsense-monologue—

> At Black heath feeld where great Golias was slain,
> The Moon lying in childebed of her last Sonne:
> The Tiborne at warwick was then King of Spain,
> By whome the land of *Canaan* then was wun . . .

—and so on for eleven quatrains. It has absolutely no significance, and (like the song) it serves to relax the spectators' minds while at the same time bringing the vice and his fellows before them. Suddenly, after a few farcical salutations, vigorous action resumes when Covetous is told that he "standeth now at the point of banishment" owing to Worldly Man's reformation. With urgent oaths he calls for his gown, cap, and chain. The suggestion that Worldly Man can be left to backslide without assistance is instantly repudiated, because a repentant sinner forthwith obtains divine forgiveness; and therefore Worldly Man must not be abandoned to his spiritual safety for a moment. The disguise is brought, and Covetous puts it on:

COUETOUSE: First to help on my gown some paines doo you take
And then I wil see what curtsie you can make.
INCONSIDERATION: It is trim indeed, by the masse in that Gown:
Me thinks you be worthy to be Mayor of a town.
COUETOUSE: Say you so? then how like you this countenaunce?
PRECIPITATION: Very comely and like a person of great gouernaunce.
COUETOUSE: Then all is wel, come, come doo your dutye:
ALL THREE: O worthy Prince Couetouse we humbly salute ye.
COUETOUSE: Body of me, that same wil marre all:
When in company I come if Couetouse you doo me call.

There is a good surprise here, when the disguise has made Covetous look respectable and the genuine homage of his fellows gives the game away. Three voices at once shout the name Covetous, and with an oath the vice instantly recalls them to the need for taking false names. These names are comically devised by Covetous (the direction bids him "study," or meditate), who complains that his thoughts are disturbed by his fellows' eagerness to know their false names, and by the presence of the spectators ("Nay, that maid looks on me"). The worldly vices—Temerity, Inconsideration, Precipitation—are to masquerade as virtues, Agility, Reason, and Ready Wit. Covetous himself is to be Policy. Thus the Worldly Man, wise in his own conceit, will rush blindly and greedily to destruction.

Covetous sends Temerity and Inconsideration out to disguise themselves ("In all the haste go thou and be thou disguised"; "Look you make you trim as fast as you can") and to acquaint themselves with Worldly Man. They never reappear. He and Precipitation (who seems to be respectably dressed enough to avoid suspicion) remain, Precipitation summing up the plot against Worldly Man until Covetous warns him that their victim approaches. "This is the worldly man I suppose indeed," says Precipitation—a necessary statement, for Worldly Man is "in a straunge attire," something sober and decent, and might not at once be recognizable. He stands "afar of," with "poorly arayed" Enough, and they expound between them a moral allegory in which covetousness is described as a chariot going on the four wheels of contempt-of-God, forgetfulness-of-death, faint-courage, and ungentleness, drawn by the two horses Raveny (rapine) and Niggardship, and driven by the carter Desire-to-have with his two-corded whip of acquisitiveness and tenacity. This is addressed to the audience, and would be readily accepted (it is obviously in the same tradition as Batman's moral picture-books; see Plates VI to X). The Worldly Man adds his own contentment with Enough, "which bringeth me to quiet in body & minde." On the other side of the "place," Covetous (in his wealthy disguise) and Precipitation prepare for a struggle, cursing Enough ("that beggerly knaue") because he is likely to stand in their way.

The temptation begins. It is both comic and sinister. Covetous surprisingly addresses himself first to Enough, and asks leave to speak privately with Worldly Man. Enough at once agrees, and there follows the direction "Let the Vice weep & houle & make great lamentation to the Worldly man." With noisy tears he poses as a well-wisher and threatens him with the reputation of a miser who renounces hospitality:

> He was wunt (saith one) to keep a good house:
> But now (saith an other) there is no liuing for a mouse.

(The echoes of Worldly Man's first speech remind us that it was before, not after, his conversion that he renounced hospitality.) It seems that Covetous may fail, and tension is kept up when Worldly Man turns to Enough as though to end this conversation, and is feverishly plucked back by Covetous:

WORLDLY MAN: He had need to liue very sircumspectly:
That would take vpon him to please all men directly.
Beholde Inough. (*Go towards him.*)
COUETOUSE: Nay hear you, this greeueth me worst so God me saue: (*Pluck him back.*)
They say you keep company with euery beggerly knaue.
WORLDLY MAN: Wher I keep company they haue nought to doo:
As neer as I can into none but honest company I go.
See you, I pray you *Inough*.
COUETOUSE: Nay but hear you, is *Inough* his name?
WORLDLY MAN: Yea indeed, it is euen the very self same.
COUETOUSE: *Saint Dunstone*, a man would not iudge it by his cote:

> Now truely I would not take him to be worth a grote.
> Hark you, hark you, in faith knowe you not me?

One can hear the stress on "me" and see the gesture with which Covetous contrasts Enough's appearance with his own. Having thus disparaged Enough, Covetous introduces himself and Precipitation as Policy and Ready Wit, chopping logic and maintaining that

> Inough is not inough without vs two:
> For hauing not vs, what can inough doo?
> Inough is maintained by wisdome and policy . . .

Precipitation argues that "enough" is relative:

> You haue no more now then dooth your self serue:
> So that your poor Breethern for all you may sterue.
> But inough that commeth by vs twain:
> Is able your self and many other to sustain:

and Worldly Man eagerly assents to the specious argument:

> Your words are euen as true as the Gospel:
> As one named Reason of late to me did tel.

Worldly reason has already, as we know, been identified as the disguise of Inconsideration. The falsity of the argument, and the sinfulness of Worldly Man's approving phrase, are brought out by Enough, who reminds us of what the Gospel actually says on this point:

> Was not the poor widdow for her offring praised more
> Then all they that offred of their superfluitie & store?

But by now Covetous's ascendancy is such that (in his gown, cap and chain) he can patronize Enough:

> He sayes wel by Lady, yea and like an honest man,
> But yet Sir, riches to be good, wel proue I can.
> For euery man is not called after one sorte: . . .
>
> Therfore euery man (as his vocation is) must walke:
> I am sure that against this you wil not talke.

In other words, if Worldly Man's vocation is to make money (which he blandly assumes it is), to lose the chance of making money is to subvert the divine scheme. The superb insolence of this, and the attentiveness of Worldly Man, cause Enough to depart with the indignant statement "The worldly man wil needs be a worldly man stil," while Covetous derides him as a deserter of his friend, and Worldly Man rejoices over what he considers a lucky escape from Enough and Contentation:

> A shame take them all, I haue spent on them xx. pound:
> That I had of money and of mine owne good ground.
> I am ashamed of my self so God me saue:
> Because I haue solde almoste all that euer I haue.

Again the hearers are invited to weigh these remarks, to note the inconsistency between the first and the fourth lines, to remember Christ's instruction to the young man of great possessions, and to mark the irony of the oath. He embraces both Covetous and Precipitation, and after a speech of self-praise by "Policy" is led out by them.

A short monologue by the Heavenly Man sums up the degeneration of Worldly Man and provides an interval before the perfected wickedness of the sinner is shown. The next person to address us is an old countryman, complaining of his rent-racking landlord ("Oh masters, is not this euen a lamentable thing?"). We guess that this landlord is Worldly Man, and so it proves:

> Chad thought a while ago my Londlord would not haue doon thus
> For he said he would be a heauenly man I wus.
> But zoule, the Deuil is as Heauenly as he:
> Three times worse then he was bevore as var as I can zee.

A servant and a hired brickmaker, from whom Worldly Man withholds board and wages respectively, add their complaints, with vigorous country rhetoric ("The dropping of his nose he would not loose"). They talk of their master's ambition, the old tenant comparing him to the Rich Fool:

> Thou foole (saith Christ) this night wil I fetch thy soule from thee:
> And then who shall haue the things that thine be?

Covetous, as steward, refuses their requests for their dues, and is supported by Worldly Man, who enters "all braue" and makes a spectacular figure. He is unmoved by their warnings that divine vengeance will fall upon him:

> Ha, ha, ha, I must laugh, so God me saue:
> To see what a sort of suters now a dayes we haue.

He is planning for the immediate, not the ultimate, future: like the Rich Fool once more, he resolves "I must make my barnes more great"; and like Ahab, he has designs on his neighbour's property, "the little tenament that by my house dooth stand." But suddenly a voice is heard:

PROPHET WITHOUT: O thou Earth, Earth, earth, hear the woord of the Lord:
Knowe thy self to be no better then Clay or dust:

(*Let the Worldly man looke sudenly about him.*)

Se that thy life to Gods trueth doo alwaies accorde:
For from earth thou cammest and to earth thou must.

The prophet Jeremiah comes in, and states that the wicked steward who misuses his master's goods will be cast into "vtter darknes." His speech is marked off from the surrounding couplets by being in two rhyme-royal stanzas. It is addressed to the hearers in general, not to Worldly Man, and its dramatic effect is that the Bible has taken human form and has walked in to denounce the evildoer. Covetous scoffs, but Worldly Man is disturbed and sends for his chaplain Devotion (really Ghostly Ignorance, mentioned by Covetous earlier in the play as a companion of his) to expound the warning.

As he awaits the return of Covetous with the chaplain, Worldly Man feels sickness coming upon him, and lies down to sleep. As he lies on the floor, *Enter Gods plague and stand behinde him a while before he speak.* God's Plague, probably wearing a devil's mask, blows upon him and strikes him with a sword; both these are symbolic acts, and like the spoken judgment on the sleeper (that he will die and receive no mercy, that his goods will perish or be dispersed, that his family will decay) they do not wake him.[7] When God's Plague goes, Covetous returns with the comic old drunkard Ghostly Ignorance. They find Worldly Man, still asleep, dreaming and calling out that he is in Hell. He wakes in agony, and Ghostly Ignorance (instead of being asked to expound the warning, for which purpose he was brought) is sent to fetch a physician. Left alone with Covetous, Worldly Man persists in thinking of his wealth, which is more real to him than his soul:

Oh policy sick, neuer so sick, oh holde my head:
Oh sira, what shal become of all my goods when I am dead?

Ghostly Ignorance returns with the Physician, who busily attends the dying man, propping him against a pillow and giving him aquavitae, while Covetous officiously fools about and calls him Flebishiten (flea-beshitten). He revives Worldly Man—who says, with terrible irony,

> You might haue let me go, I was wel out of my pain—

but warns him that he must prepare to die. Worldly Man's response is astonishing:

> Go thy waies I pray thee and trouble not my minde:
> For these newes, to giue thee any thing, in my hart I cannot finde.

And, the Physician indignantly gone, the dying man devises frauds against his creditors: his estate is to be kept intact, even though he has enough to pay every man his due. Next he prepares to make a will, with Ghostly Ignorance as scribe:

> IGNORANCE: Heer is Ink and Paper, what shall I write?
> WORLDLY MAN: In the name, first of all doo thou indite.
> IGNORANCE: In the name, in, in, in, in the name, what more?
> WORLDLY MAN: Of.
> IGNORANCE: Of, of, of, what more?[8](*fall down.*)
> COUETOUSE: Body of me, down with the paper, away with the Ink:
> IGNORANCE: Passion of me Couetouse he is gone me think.
> Holde, holde him, let vs see if any life in him be:
> COUETOUSE: Nay holde him that will, the Deuil holde him for me.

The dramatic tension of this race against death is not incompatible with the sinister comedy. Along with the solemn satisfaction that God will not permit his name to be used in a wicked will, there goes a derisive satisfaction that Worldly Man's sins have recoiled upon him. The scribal fumblings of the priest, and the off-hand yet significant phrase with which the vice drops the corpse, play their part in producing this mixed response to the scene.

This is not the end of the play. The corpse (still "all braue" in its dress) is abandoned, a grotesque and yet a pitiable object, to the spectators' reflections. The actor of Ghostly Ignorance is meanwhile changing his costume and will soon reappear. There breaks in upon these reflections the sound of roaring, and Satan comes in:

> Oh, oh, oh, oh, all is mine, all is mine . . .

He speaks the final judgment on Worldly Man:

> The worldly man (quoth he) nay the diuilish man than . . .

(since the play has been built round the antithesis of the worldly and the heavenly, this phrase is a dramatic surprise; for all the earlier talk of heaven and hell, a deeper gulf seems to open). Satan is confident, radiant with infernal hospitality. He pays tribute to the genius of Covetous and to that of the Worldly Man himself. He offers a smiling invitation:

> All you worldly men, that in your riches doo trust,
> Be mery and iocond, builde Palaces and make lusty cheer:
> Put your money to Usury, let it not lye and rust,
> Occupye your selues in my lawes while ye be heer.
> Spare not, nor care not, what mischeef you frequent,
> Use drunkennes, deceit, take other mens wiues:
> Passe of nothing, one houre is inough to repent,
> Of all the wickednes you haue doon in your liues.
> Oh if you wil thus after my Lawes behaue,
> You shall haue all things as this worldly man had:
> Be bolde of me, what you wil to craue,
> And dout you not but with you I wil play the loouing lad.
> Yea, and after death I wil prouide a place,
> For you in my kingdome for euer to reign:
> You shall fare no wurse then dooth mine owne grace,
> That is to lye burning for euer in pain.

As the spectators recoil, he turns back with a shrug to the corpse, addressing it as though it were still alive, and thus providing a terrible reminder that the soul lives still:

> Come on mine owne Boy, go thou with me,
> Thou hast serued me duely, and hatest me neuer:
> Therfore now for thy paines rewarded shalt thou be:
> In euer lasting fire that burneth for euer.
> (*Bear him out vpon his back.*)

After another short pause, Contentation, Enough, and the Heavenly Man enter together (the player of Satan reappearing as Contentation). In weighty stanzas of rhyme-royal they contrast the unquiet life and death of the Worldly Man with the tranquillity of the Heavenly Man. This tranquillity is personified as Rest; he now comes in to reward the Heavenly Man, who thanks God for the great gift (perhaps symbolized by a crown). With this the action ends, and there follow the customary prayers for the Queen and all her subjects:

> Inough is as good as a feast, heer let vs stay,
> We haue troubled our audience, that let vs remember:

Let vs conclude therfore, but first let vs pray,
That it wil please God in mercy our good mistres to tender,
Our faith to stablish wherin we be slender.
That at the last day when the trump shall blowe:
For to be heauenly men the Lord may vs al knowe.

Liberality and Prodigality

This interlude, "As it was playd before her Maiestie," begins with a scenic effect. The spectators have before them a "place" backed by various structures—an inn (perhaps two), some simple dwelling, and in the centre a splendid palace two storeys high, decorated with careful craftsmanship. There is no curtain to conceal this scenery, which arouses interest and speculation before the play begins.

One of the boys who are acting the play enters to speak the prologue. It is a prologue which keeps up expectation by systematically concealing the play's subject, saying only what it is *not*: the matter will be neither theological, not historical, nor political, nor philosophical, nor scurrilously farcical;

But this we bring, is but to serue the time,
A poore deuice, to passe the day withall:
To loftier points of skill we dare not clime,
Lest perking ouer-hie, with shame wee fall.
  Such as doth best beseeme such as we be,
  Such we present, and craue your courtesie.

Assured that there is no offence in the argument, the court can settle down to this pastime. Immediately Vanity, dressed in multicoloured feathers, swaggers out from the palace and introduces himself by explaining the meaning of his costume:

And so I am, to put you out of doubt,
Euen Vanitie wholly, within, without,
In head, in heart, in all parts round about:

(marking the last line of the triplet with a pirouette and an obeisance of graceful familiarity). He has come to prepare the arrival of Fortune, his "most soueraigne dame":

Here will she mount this stately sumptuous throne,
As she is wont to heare each mans desire:
And whoso winnes her fauour by his mone,
May haue of her, the thing he doth require.

He condescendingly mentions her adversary Virtue, who is little prized and will occupy "this other seate":

> But 'twixt their states, what difference will be,
> Your selues shall iudge, and witnesse when you see.[9]

He goes into the palace, and the spectators are left looking at the two "houses" he has just indicated, wondering which of the rival goddesses will first appear.

Instead of either, an over-dressed gallant bursts in, with a resentful postilion in tow. The gallant insists on halting at the inn before them, though the postilion warns him that the Host is a known swindler and reminds him that they have only six more miles of their journey to go. They knock and call loudly, until at last the Host appears; then they have hard work to persuade him to take them in:

> HOST: Nay, soft a while, I am not wont so late
> To take in ghests; I like ye not: away.
> PROD.: Nay, stay awhile, mine host, I pray thee stay,
> Open the gate, I pray thee heartily,
> And what we take, we will pay thee royally.
> HOST: And would ye haue lodging then?
> PROD.: Yea rather then my life.
> HOST: Then stay a while, ile first goe aske my wife.

(popping his head in again). Soon he reappears and resumes his catechism, maddeningly, from first principles:

> Then you would haue lodging, belike sir?
> PROD.: Yea, I pray thee come quickly.
> HOST: What's your name, and please you?
> PROD.: Prodigalitie.
> HOST: And will you indeed spend lustily?
> PROD.: Yea that I will.
> HOST: And take that ye finde, patiently?
> PROD.: What els?
> HOST: And pay what I aske, willingly?
> PROD.: Yea, all reckonings, vnreasonably.
> HOST: Well, goe to, for this once I am content to receyue ye:
> Come on, sir, I dare say, you are almost wearie.
> PROD: Thou maist sweare it.

They go in, and Virtue and Equity appear. Virtue speaks in rhetorical alexandrines, reminiscent of *Tottel's Miscellany*:

> Oh most vnhappie state, of recklesse humane kinde!
> Oh dangerous race of man, vnwitty, fond, and blinde!

Oh wretched worldlings, subiect to all misery,
When fortune is the proppe of your prosperitie!

This is not really addressed to the audience, but amounts to a statement that there is opposition between Virtue and Fortune. Virtue, as a character, is not important in the play; her superiority to Fortune is not enforced but assumed.[10] The purposes of this speech are to introduce her, to install her in her "homely bowre," and to separate the arrival of Prodigality from that of old Tenacity, who now trudges in wearily, bound for Fortune's palace, and pulling after him an artificial ass (presumably on wheels). The ass is lean and Tenacity is corpulent. The sprightly Vanity, who meets Tenacity from the palace, forms another contrast with the fat old countryman, and ridicules "this Coystrell" in asides to the audience. Vanity re-enters the palace and Tenacity finds lodging at the inn.

There next enters Money, a small boy in a costume covered all over with silver-paper coins. He introduces himself by means of a song, and then (as Vanity joins him) announces Fortune:

VAN.: But, Money, of Fortune our soueraigne dame,
What newes?
MON.: Marry sir, of purpose I hither came,
To let thee know she will forth-with be here:
And loe, alreadie see she doth appeare.
VAN.: Tis true; now must I shew my diligence.
Downe Ladies, stowpe, do your reuerence.
(*Enter Fortune in her Chariot drawne with Kings.*)

Vanity's command, of course, is addressed to Elizabeth's ladies and waiting-women: it awakens attention and also arouses opposition to Fortune. Fortune has a "trayne" attending on her, and the burden of their song—"Reuerence, due reuerence, fair dames do reuerence"—strikes just the right note of mingled imperiousness and compliment. Fortune's speech is eloquent, suiting the splendour of her entrance:

I doubt not, but by this my pompous shew,
By vestures wrought with gold so gorgeously,
By reuerence done to me of high and lowe,
By all these ornaments of brauerie,
By this my trayne that now attends me so,
By Kings that hale my Chariot to and fro,
Fortune is knowne the Queene of al renowne,
That makes, that marres, sets vp, and throwes adowne.

She proceeds to her "stately throne," and the attendants again sing as she ascends it.

Though the play is divided into acts and scenes, the action seems to be continuous (scene-divisions merely mark the arrival of fresh characters); and the speech of Liberality, II. i, is complementary to Fortune's boast. Liberality declares that the coming trial of strength will establish Virtue's supremacy. Rewards must be given according to virtue, especially in public life:

> Where any well deserue, and are rewarded well,
> There Prince and people both, in safety sure do dwell.
> Where he that truly serues, hath nothing for his paine,
> More hearts are lost, then pecks of gold can ransome home agayne.

This is of course relevant to Elizabeth's responsibilities, but it is not, I think, presented as a warning but as a truism. The point will be returned to later; in the meantime, Liberality retires as he sees Tenacity coming. Tenacity is demonstrating, in pun and gesture, his weariness; he is on foot

> For Brocke mine Asse is saddle-pincht vull sore,
> And so am I, euen here: chill say no more.

He encounters Vanity (entering from Fortune's palace as Tenacity approaches it), who accepts with gravity the promise of a bribe of three-halfpence, and (as before) mocks the miser in asides. By Vanity's design Tenacity is delayed till Prodigality also appears. There is the expected quarrel, leading straight on to Vanity's presenting of the suitors to Fortune, who seems to be discovered above in the palace. For greater variety, both suitors sing characteristic songs, with Tenacity amusingly warming to the work and eager to go on after a halt has been called. When Money has been entrusted to Prodigality, Tenacity departs (Vanity encouraging him with the idea that his turn will soon come), and the winner sings again in praise of Fortune and Money.

A continuous episode now leads to Prodigality's loss of Money. First Dandaline the hostess, then Tom Toss and Dick Dicer the gamesters, are seen laying their plans to entrap him. The speech of Dandaline (a feminine "character" part) is carefully designed to display the boy actor's talents, starting with a burst of indignation against a servant off-stage—

> Now Ifaith ye little peeuish harlotrie,
> Ile one day make you spit your meate more handsomly—

then falling into conversation with the spectators about the servant's mistake (trying to roast a fowl and a joint at the same spit), proceeding to advertiser's patter—

> A better bird, a fairer bird, a finer bird,
> A sweeter bird, a yonger bird, a tenderer bird,
> A daintier bird, (*etc.*)—

next assuming a conspiratorial tone (she will over-charge her guest), and finishing with innuendo (a pun on "lemon" and "lemman"). The dialogue between Prodigality and the gamesters, ending with a song ("some sweet roysting harmony"), leads to a flaunting exit with gold tassels waving: *Exeunt. Flie gold knops.*

Up to this point we have been shown Fortune's capriciousness. Now Virtue's discrimination appears, in a scene where Liberality promises to reward the merit of Captain Well-done but tells an importunate Courtier that he must serve longer than "a yeare or twaine" before he gets preferment. Liberality's introductory speech is in the impersonal generalized manner that is the play's occasional weakness:

> The more a man with vertuous dealing doth himselfe invre,
> The lesse with worldly businesse, he is molested sure . . . (*etc.*)

His dialogue with the suitors, however, brings the audience back into the play. The Courtier serves as secretary to "a noble man neere about her Maiesty," the Captain has served in the Queen's wars. There is compliment in the Captain's recognition that his lack of advancement is due to ill destiny, "For well I know, the Prince is full of liberalitie."

This scene has also served to fill the interval during which Prodigality has fallen to extravagance, and we are recalled to that story by Money's effective entrance:

> Libertie, libertie, now I cry libertie:
> Catch me againe when you can, Prodigalitie.

He runs in with his clothes in rags, "spoyled" and "like a new shorne sheepe," as he confides to the spectators:

> And though I haue bin pinched very neere,
> I am glad to see you in good health euery one here:

And now I haue escaped the traiterous treachery
Of such a thriftlesse Roysting company,
To my mother in haste againe I will get me,
And keepe at home safely: from thence let them fet me.

And pausing only to exchange a few indignant words with Vanity (who emerges from the palace as Money goes in) he vanishes. Almost as soon as he has gone, Tenacity appears again, and we know that now it is his turn to entertain Money. Vanity once more trifles with him, exhibiting him to the audience, ironically expressing a fear that Tenacity will spend Money too fast, and then enquiring what he means to do with Money:

TEN.: Chud, chud, chud, chud.
VAN.: Chud, chud, what chud?
TEN.: Chud doe no harme at all.
VAN.: No, nor much good (I thinke) to great nor small.

The purpose of this dialogue is not moral exposure but entertainment. Prodigality and Tenacity are both presented as absurd eccentrics: neither has any social reality. Tenacity is never shown grinding the faces of the poor, or devouring them like bread; and when he dies, he has no spiritual future either in Heaven or in Hell. Tenacity is awarded the custody of Money, and promptly ties him up, "Vor veare of robbing by the high way" (this helps us foresee the outcome). *Here Tenacity goeth to the Inne for his Asse. Exit.* The direction implies that he fetches the ass on stage again, and then takes the road with the ass and Money at his heels: it marks his final departure from Fortune's palace.

No sooner is he gone than Prodigality enters, cursing his luck and hunting for Money. Accompanied by Dick Dicer, he marches to the palace and commands Vanity (who, I think, speaks from above, as he is certainly out of reach) to bear a message to Fortune:

Therefore charge her in the name of Prodigality,
That he be restored to me incontinently,
Lest she repent it.
VAN.: These be sore and cruell threatnings, marry.
Is your haste so great, that by no meanes you may tarry?
PROD.: I will not tarry, and therefore make haste.
VAN.: Soft, sir, a little, there is no time past.
You may tarry, you must tarry, for ought as I know:
Nay, then you shall tarry, whether you wil or no. (*Exit.*)
DICK: Swounds, sir, he mocks you.
PROD.: Gibe not with me, you hoorson raskall slaue

For money I come, and money will I haue.
Sirra, Vanity, Vanity. What, Vanity?
Speake and be hang'd, Vanity. What wil't not be?

He continues to shout, but receives no answer. Fortune and Vanity are seen above, unknown to him, tying a noose in a rope. Below, Prodigality and Dicer set a ladder against the wall. *Here Prod. scaleth. Fortune claps a halter about his neck, he breaketh the halter & falles*. Prodigality rages at Fortune:

I abhorre the, I defie thee, wheresoeuer I go,
I doe proclaime my selfe thy mortall foe.

The phrase is absurdly equivalent to calling down ill-luck upon himself, and, like Vanity's opinion that

The Gentleman will neuer hold himselfe quiet,
Till once more he come to taste of this dyet,

it foretells his future career, which Fortune now resolves to blight:

He shall arriue vnto a wretched end,
And with repentance learne how to offend
A goddesse of my state and dignitie.

So saying, Fortune descends from her throne and makes a processional exit in her chariot, her attendants singing as before:

VAN.: Madam, here are your vassals ready prest,
To doe the thing that Fortune liketh best.
FOR.: Well then, come on, to witnes this our victorie,
Depart we hence with sound of fame triumphantly.
(*Reuerence, due reuerence.*)

As this splendid procession leaves (marking Fortune's departure from the action) a disreputable one appears: Prodigality, Toss and Dicer hurry in, with Money bound as their captive.[11] Money has grown swollen in Tenacity's keeping (presumably his costume is stuffed with cushions and the like), and instead of keeping pace "He falles downe vpon his elbow." There is not only an amusing satirical effect here, at the expense of usury and of prodigality (the revellers propose a course of physic guaranteed to make Money lean again), but a dramatic one: as Prodigality urges Money to exert himself—"Come vp, gentle Money, wee may not here stay"—we ask ourselves what has happened to Tenacity. The answer is supplied directly: *The Constables make hue and cry,* calling up the Host and his servants to pursue the murderers of the old miser.

The end of the play now draws near. There is another formal statement, in fourteeners carved up between Virtue and Equity, that a reasonable being like man should incline to virtue, since the greatest pleasure consists therein. A song makes the point, and adds decoration to the scene. As Virtue is preparing to leave the stage, Liberality brings in the Sheriff, who has with him Money (still bound and swollen). The murder is related and Money entrusted to Liberality, who immediately gives Captain Well-done a hundred crowns and also rewards two other deserving suitors. Though Liberality is Virtue's steward, his words "Hold, pray for the Queen," and the response "God saue the Queene, and God saue Liberalitie" make it clear that rewards come from Elizabeth. Perhaps, indeed, each rewarded suitor makes obeisance to the Queen in the audience. Tipstaves now enter, turning the acting-space into a court of justice: "Roome, my Masters, giue place, stand by." Prodigality is indicted (in prose, and according to the form of law) of the robbery and murder, to which he pleads guilty, and for which he is sentenced (again in the legal formula) to death. He now makes a repentant statement:

I finde the brittle stay of trustlesse Fortunes state.
My heart now thirsteth after Vertue, all too late:
Yet good my Lord, of pittie condiscend,
To be a meane for him, that meaneth to amend.
The Prince is mercifull, of whose great mercy,
Full many haue largely tasted already:
Which makes me appeale thereto more boldly.

IUDG.: Prodigalitie, I not mislike your wailefull disposition,
And therefore, for you to the Prince, there shall be made Petition,
That though your punishment be not fully remitted,
Yet in some part, it may be qualified.

PROD.: God saue your life.

(*Vertue, Equitie, Liberalitie, Iudge, and all come downe before the Queene, and after reuerence made, Vertue speaketh.*)

THE EPILOGVE.

Most mightie Queene, yonder I sate in place,
Presenting shew of chiefest dignitie;
Here prostrate, lo, before your Princely grace,
I shew my selfe, such as I ought to be,

> Your humble vassall, subiect to your will,
> With feare and loue, your Grace to reuerence still.

The speaker of the epilogue is named as Virtue, but the lines are more appropriate to Fortune, who has in fact been enthroned during the play. I imagine that the whole cast, not merely those playing in this final scene, appear to do homage at the end.

Here again it is the spectacular compliment that justifies the scene.[12] Nobody can feel much concern at Prodigality's condemnation, any more than at Tenacity's death; pity and triumph are equally inappropriate to either occasion. (Wager's treatment of Worldly Man's death is intentionally quite different.) The play is not, and is not intended to be, anything more than an entertaining and decorative spectacle seasoned with polite flattery. Its effectiveness is almost entirely dependent on its being performed with skill in the right circumstances. It is, of course, in consequence a much less substantial piece than *Enough is as good as a Feast*; it is wholly lacking, for example, in the powerful moral ironies of Wager's play. It would be hard to find two so different plays written so close together on so similar a theme. The real nature of these two Tudor interludes, and of all others, can be brought out only by considering them as plays written for actors to perform and audiences to watch.

NOTES

INTRODUCTION

1. 1. J. A. Symonds, *Shakespeare's Predecessors* (1900 edn.), 118–9. Compare A. Nicoll, *British Drama* (1947 edn.), 57: "The real service of the authors of these plays (*Apius and Virginia, Calisto and Melibea, Damon and Pithias, Fulgens and Lucrece*), however, to the development of the drama lies in the driving away of the extraneous 'moral' and the consequent disappearance of abstract types and characters." A. S. Downer, *The British Drama: a handbook and brief chronicle* (1950, New York), 51: "tedious lectures are delivered at frequent intervals by allegorical commentators." Rossiter, *English Drama*, 105: "Tudor interludes do show some slight fear of boring their audience—though *we* may wonder much rather at our ancestors' astonishing *endurance*!—and from that laudable weakness comes, in time, a totally non-instructive kind of entertainment . . ." (the plays of John Heywood).

2. 2. F. S. Boas and A. W. Reed, Oxford, 1926, xxii.

3. 3. Roper's *Life and Death of Sir Thomas More*, quoted by Chambers, *M.S.*, II, 193 note.

CHAPTER I

7. 1. My account is particularly indebted to his *Medieval Stage*, chapter XXII, and to his *Elizabethan Stage*, chapter XIX.

7. 2. Chambers, *M.S.*, II, 136.

7. 3. *Two Coventry Corpus Christi Plays*, ed. H. Craig, 27 (the Shearmen and Tailors' Pageant).

8. 4. *Ludus Coventriae*, ed. K. S. Block, 230, 232, 245.

8. 5. An example by Pieter Bruegel the Younger (1564–1637) is in the Fitzwilliam Museum, Cambridge. The title is *A Village Fête*, and the picture, painted in 1632 (possibly after an original by Pieter Bruegel the Elder), is one of many variants. Similar stages are shown in A. Nicoll, *Development of the Theatre*, figs. 64 and 65 (France, early sixteenth century). For further discussion of the trestle stage, see C. Walter Hodges, *The Globe Restored* (1953).

8. 6. Chambers, *E.S.*, III, 26 note 3, quotes Puttenham's description of the classical stage (1589). Puttenham, who probably derived his knowledge from such woodcut illustrations of arcade screens as appear in the fifteenth-century editions of Terence, writes of "sundrie little diuisions by curteins as trauerses to serue for seueral roomes where they might repaire vnto and change their garments and come in againe, as their speaches and parts were to be renewed."

9. 7. For details of such Tudor halls, see J. A. Gotch, *The Growth of the English House*, 95, and H. A. Tipping, *English Homes*, II, 52, 246, 250.

9. 8. A. J. Mill, *Medieval Plays in Scotland*, 291. The plays of Thomas Ashton, who became headmaster of Shrewsbury in 1561, were performed by the boys in the Quarry there, which seems to have been a natural amphitheatre: T. H. V. Motter, *The School Drama in England*, 207 *et seq*.

9. 9. J. W. Harris, *John Bale*, 101–3. On the Kilkenny performance, 45, 103–4.

10. 10. When Flatterie, Falset, and Dissait take false names each undergoes a mock baptism with real water. The Sowter's Wife begins to wade across the stream, but changes her mind. Falset and Dissait run away through the water after stealing the king's treasure. The Poor Man throws the Pardoner's relics into the water. Discussions of the performances of 1552 and 1554 are to be found in Hamer's edition of Lyndsay's *Works*, IV, 126 *et seq*., 153 *et seq*., and in an article by A. J. Mill, *P.M.L.A.*, 1932, 636 *et seq*. The play was originally (1540) in the form of a short indoor interlude: a witness's description is printed by Hamer, II, 1. On the lost Scottish plays mentioned in this paragraph, see A. J. Mill, *Medieval Plays in Scotland*, 291.

10. 11. Chambers, *E.S.*, III, 23. That John Heywood's *Johan Johan*, an adaptation of the French *Farce du Pasté*, was intended for this indoor setting is made plain by Tyb's interpolated threat to throw a shovelful of coals at her husband: this shows that Heywood, unlike the author of his source, could count on a real hearth (see my article on the play, *M.L.R.*, XLV, 1950, 295 note).

10. 12. From John Palsgrave's denial, in the prologue to *Acolastus* (1540), "that we wold for our new inuentions dryue the comedies of Plautus and Terence frome the hyghe deasse, downe behynde the skryne," it appears that a staged dais might occasionally be used, unless the image is wholly figurative (the original Latin has merely "*velut simul de ponte deiectis*"). Chambers notes that the staged dais was a rarity: *E.S.*, III, 23; I, 228–9.

10. 13. Chambers, *E.S.* III, 35 note 1. His suggestions about the "houses" required will be discussed later, in note 35 to p. 17.

11. 14. When Money is to vomit up Pleasure, "there must be a chayre for him to sit in, and vnder it or neere the same there must be some hollowe place for one to come vp in." The birth takes place as follows: "money shal make as though he would vomit, and with some fine conueyance pleasure shall appeare from beneath, and lie there apparelled." It may be noted that when Judas and Dives come "in," and are driven "out" by Damnation, they do not rise from a subterranean Hell.

11. 15. Machyn, *Diary, 1550–63* (1848), 222, 275. The former was in an unnamed hall (perhaps that of the company to which the Lord Mayor, whose procession to St Paul's had just been related, belonged), the latter "in the quen hall at Westmynster" for a play by the gentlemen of the Temple. For the Cambridge stage see G. C. M. Smith (ed.), "The Academic Drama at Cambridge: Extracts from College

Records" in Malone Society's *Collections*, II, ii. 163. Carpenters were paid at Queens' College, Cambridge, in 1547 and again in 1548 for services "ad le skrene et ad theatrum" (*ibid.*, II, ii. 229, 185).

11. 16. On the staging of *The Cobbler's Prophecy* see below, p. 17, note 35. There are a few indications that a constructed stage background is wanted in *Apius and Virginia*. When Virginius says to Apius

> If ought I haue offended you, your Courte, or eke your Crowne,
> From lofty top of Turret hie, persupetat me downe

he may point to a constructed palace ("persupetat"=precipitate). But the incident which principally suggests some background other than two screen doors is that in which Apius becomes aware of Conscience and Justice. Having resolved to gain Virginia by force, he says

> I finde it, I minde it, I sweare that I will,
> Though shame, or defame, do happen, no skill;
> But out I am wounded, how am I deuided?
> Two states of my life, from me are now glided,
> For Consience he pricketh me contempned,
> And Iustice saith, Iudgement wold haue me condemned.

Alongside this speech is the marginal direction:

> Here let him make as thogh he went out and let Consince and Iustice come out of him, and let Consience hold in his hande a Lamp burning and let Iustice haue a sworde and hold it before Apius brest.

It seems that they glide out from an entrance at the back of the stage, this entrance being masked by Apius as he turns away from the audience towards it. They are obviously meant to appear to issue from his body. Later his dying Conscience pleads with him once more not to ravish Virginia ("here let Consience speake within") and he cries "Whence doth this pinching sounde desende?" "Desende" is probably used for its rhyme with "end," and I do not suppose that Conscience spoke from above, but his rhymed speeches must have been fully audible, and this could not be relied upon if he spoke outside a real door.

11. 17. Chambers, *E.S.* III, 25.

11. 18. In *Patient Grissell* a messenger goes "once or twise about the Staige" when he is supposed to cover a considerable distance. In *The Marriage of Wit and Wisdom* Idleness leads Wit to the den of Irksomeness. He also must compass the stage a few times during the process, for it covers a costume-change (from Honest Recreation to Irksomeness).

12. 19. "We shal be at Ierusalem, I think, to morow." There is a real, though smaller, compression of distance later in the play, during the banquet; Mary, in soliloquy, resolves to "seeke" Christ at Simon's house, and directly proceeds thither.

12. 20. Simon takes Christ out to walk in his garden (offstage) while Malicious Judgment is to "make all thyngs ready." The vice assists ("Helpe to make all ready, and the cloth to lay": the laying of the cloth is

second). Simon orders a stool and a cushion to be set for Christ. The banquet ended, Simon says "Syrs, take away here, we will no more now," but the clearing away is still unfinished 160 lines later:

> Away with this geare, how long shall we syt here?
> At once: We haue somewhat els to do I thinke.

12. 21. Chambers, *E.S.*, III, 25.

12. 22. The son's wife commands him "styrre not for any thynge out of my doore." But the action is not consistently inside the house, for the son is sent on errands by his wife and returns "home" from them. One of these errands is discussed later in this chapter, p. 26.

13. 23. There was already established, as Chambers notes (*E.S.*, III, 23), the tradition of associating one door with a particular place. In *The Four Elements* the tavern is "at the dore euyn here by"; the door is not, I think, representing the tavern door itself, but is the means whereby characters leave for the tavern. In Redford's *Wit and Science* one door is associated with Tediousness. He "cumth in" as Wit and his supporters go out, *l.* 145. After a speech he sits down, and then "Wyt spekyth at the doore" (the door at which Wit went out), enters and fights him. Study and Diligence flee, and Tediousness clubs Wit and then retires to his "owne nest" (departs by his door). These movements are repeated at the second combat, of which Instruction says to Wit "To mark it in deede heere wyll I abyde"—at the door of their entrance, while Wit and his other allies proceed to the other door and "the feend is raysyd." Finally Tediousness is driven "in" (to his door), and slain offstage. Some realism may have been attempted in decorating Tediousness's door: see below, p. 14, note 26.

13. 24. Chambers (*E.S.*, III, 24–5) has suggested that "houses" are required for *Jacob and Esau, The Marriage of Wit and Wisdom, Misogonus, The Conflict of Conscience, Three Ladies of London*, and also (III, 28) for *Tom Tyler* and (III, 38) *Patient Grissell.* In some of these plays I believe that no "houses" are required; in others, fewer than Chambers postulates.

(*i*) *Jacob and Esau.* Chambers states that three tents—of Jacob, Esau, and Isaac—are wanted. But the plural form "tents" occurs seldom and is soon entirely replaced by the singular "tent," and it becomes clear that "the tent" houses Isaac and his wife, sons, and servants, while "the tents" refers to the settlement as a whole and includes dwellings of Hanan, Zethar, and other neighbours. Thus Rebecca, speaking to Isaac, praises Jacob who "liueth here quietly at home in the Tent," but condemns Esau because he goes out so early and "returneth home againe" so late that the neighbours sometimes ask her if he is still alive (*i.e.*, he lives with Isaac and Rebecca). Only the comic Ragau is a personal servant (to Esau), the others belonging to the whole family; and Esau bids Ragau "Then go see all be well in my parte of the tent." Against the weight of this evidence the marginal direction "Esau entring into Iacobs tent shaketh Ragau off" is insignificant: perhaps the tent is called Jacob's because his pottage is there (he has earlier called it his "little cottage," obviously for the sake of the rhyme). The play could in fact be staged without scenery, but I think a "house" representing "the tent," with Isaac's bench standing before it, is desirable.

(*ii*) *Misogonus*. Chambers notes that "there is one scene, in Melissa's 'bowre' (II. 4, 12) which must somehow have been represented." But though the scene is there (she has invited Misogonus thither two scenes earlier), the opening words of Misogonus, "Come one, my swete harte," show that they walk on, the "place" becoming the bower by virtue of Melissa's presence (compare Simon's house in *Mary Magdalene*, above, p. 12). There is, admittedly, no mention of the bringing on of table or chairs for the gaming which follows, as there is for Simon's banquet, but portable properties might easily be brought on by the characters who were to use them. There is a similar gaming scene, supposedly in a tavern, in *The Nice Wanton*, during which Iniquity "casteth dice on the bord"; and this board, like whatever is used for the gaming in *Misogonus*, is the only stage property required.

(*iii*) *The Conflict of Conscience* and

(*iv*) *Three Ladies of London*. Chambers states that the open "place" is converted suddenly into a court of justice in the fourth act of *The Conflict of Conscience* and the last scene of *Three Ladies of London*. With this I agree, with the proviso that since *The Conflict of Conscience* contains no other localized scenes, the necessary furniture for the court-scene may have remained throughout (there is certainly no provision either for its introduction or removal). Chambers also suggests, I think wrongly, that "two houses in London itself" form the visual background of *Three Ladies of London*. This does not take into account the two scenes in Turkey which feature the Italian merchant, and which demand the absence of scenery localizing the action in London. The second of these scenes, incidentally, is in another court of justice, but there is no indication or need of court-room furniture; whereas in the final scene there are seats for the judge and clerk and a "barre" for the prisoners, and a transition to a public theatre's inner stage is perhaps desirable (the original title-page has the phrase "as it hath been publiquely played"). In one scene Lucre's gate is suggested by one of the stage-doors (Simplicity and the professional beggars go to her "gate," her porter Fraud enters and complains of their "bauling so at my Ladies doore"), but neither her house nor that of Love and Conscience can have been represented. When characters leave the stage they are merely setting off for one or the other house, not entering its doors. Love invites Conscience "to walke home from this company." Lucre bids her new steward Dissimulation "to my Pallas haste thee awaie" to order a feast for himself and his friends, but adds

> But staie Dissimulation, I my selfe will go with thee.
> Gentlemen Ile goe before, but pray in any case:
> So soone as ye please resorte to my place.

She later enters to meet Conscience, with "Me thought I heard one cry bromes along the dore," and soon commands Usury to "carrie in" the brooms and "steppe in" to fetch the box of abomination; but none of these means more than that her house is adjacent to the stage, being either represented by one of the doors (on the occasion when Fraud is porter thereat) or imagined to be somewhere outside the door.

(*v*) *The Marriage of Wit and Wisdom*. Chambers says that action takes place "at the entrances of the house of Wantonness, of the den of Irksomeness, of a prison, and of Mother Bee's house, and the prison, as commonly in plays of later types, must have been so arranged as to allow a prisoner to take part in the dialogue from within. Some realism, also, in the treatment of the den may be signified by the allusion to 'these craggie clifts'." But of these only the prison (used for one episode) is put to any practical use comparable with that of Dame Chat's house in *Gammer Gurton's Needle*. The prison would repay construction, but the others are far more likely to have been successively imagined and forgotten: all could have been represented by the same door. "These craggie cliftes" is Wisdom's phrase for the vantage-point from which she sees the fight: it is merely a reminiscence of Mount Parnassus in Redford's *Wit and Science*, and she does not descend but "enters" for this and her other speeches.

(*vi*) *Tom Tyler*. Chambers says that "there is at one point (512) a transition from exterior to interior action. Hitherto it has been in front of Tom's house; now it is within, and his wife is in bed. An open *loggia* here hardly meets the case. The bed demands some discovery, perhaps by the withdrawal of a curtain." It is possible that Tom's house is a structure large enough for visible action to take place inside it, the front being a withdrawable curtain. But if so, this would (I think) be the only interlude employing this elaborate stage-setting. (Where "houses" are used elsewhere, it is as a background to exterior action: characters go into houses and come out, but action is not shown within.) In fact there seems to be only limited space, as the spectators are asked to make "room" for the players (*l.* 18). It seems most probable, since the events of the play (a simple domestic farce) are quite clear, that the whole stage was inside or outside Tom's house as each episode required, the transition being marked not by the movements of the characters but by their statements. It may even be wondered whether the bed was real or imaginary. It is mentioned at *l.* 505, and Tom sees his wife in bed when he comes home, *l.* 520; but in lying down, Tom's wife simply says "I will take a nap / If I can where I lie" (*ll.* 514–5), which resembles her earlier instruction to her gossips "Sit down even here, and fall to it there," *l.* 150. If the bed was real, it could either have been revealed behind a curtain or pushed forward from behind one. No provision is made for its removal or concealment when the action has become exterior again and Tom's wife bids him "Come home, or I will fetch you" (*l.* 777). A curtained background is perhaps desirable, as a song off-stage is audible at the end ("Here they all go in, and one cometh out, and singeth this Song following all alone with instruments, and all the rest within sing, between every staffe, the first two lines").

(*vii*) *Patient Grissell.* According to Chambers, this play "requires two localities. The more important is Salucia (Saluzzo), where are Gautier's mansion, Janickell's cottage, and the house of Mother Apleyarde, a midwife (*l.* 1306). The other is Bullin Lagras (Bologna), where there are two short episodes (*ll.* 1235–92, 1877–1900) at the house of the Countess of Pango. There can be little doubt that all the *domus* were staged at once. There is direct transfer of action from Gautier's to the cottage and back again (*ll.* 612–34; *cf.* 1719, 2042, 2090). Yet there is some little distance between, for when a messenger is sent, the foreshortening of space is indicated by the stage-direction (*l.* 1835) 'Go once or twise about the Staige'. Similarly, unless an 'Exiunt' has dropped out, there is direct transfer (*l.* 1900) from Bullin Lagras to Salucia." The only buildings which are put to theatrical use (*e.g.*, when a character speaks to another character who is within and comes out, like Science from her house in *The Marriage of Wit and Science*) are Janickell's cottage and Mother Apleyarde's: the latter has a real door at which Politic Persuasion knocks (*l.* 1306); and when Gautier sends Grissell for her father, she is speaking to him in the following line (*ll.* 619–20). This does not, however, mean that Chambers's instances of direct action need be accepted: Gautier, when he sends Grissell for Janickell, is not at his palace but standing in the "place," for Grissell tells Janickell that she met him "comming by the way" and that he "stayeth hereby" (*ll.* 624, 629). The same may be said of Chambers's other instances. There is no necessity that Grissell's entry at *l.* 1701 shall be from the palace, and Gautier's speeches at *ll.* 2042 and 2090 merely reveal his intention to enter his palace, not the entry itself. The palaces are never mentioned in the directions, which indicate only entrances and exits, these often making direct transfer impossible (*e.g.*, the "Exit" at *l.* 1279, when Diligence leaves the Countess of Pango and returns to Salucia). On the other hand, though the palace is not required by the action, there is no reason why it should not be gratuitously shown: indeed, since the two cottages must have been *domus*, and one of them (Mother Apleyarde's) is put to very brief use, it would be consistent and decoratively desirable to represent Gautier's palace (perhaps even the Countess of Pango's, though just before she and her maid "Exiunt" they merely announce their intention to "departe this place" and do not talk of entering a palace, *ll.* 1291–2). The fact remains that if these palaces were shown, the setting differs from those of the other court plays, being merely decorative where those were functional.

14. 25. Chambers, *E.S.*, III, 27, 38, speculates on the nature of the "post" by which Gammer Gurton sits in this play, and against which characters are threatened with being bumped in *Cambises* and *Jack Juggler*. He seems to imagine a post standing in isolation; but surely a door-post is meant?

14. 26. Hall's *Chronicle* (ed. Ellis, 1809), 580. Such a representational wood may have been used for Tediousness's entrances in Redford's *Wit and Science*, for the staging of which see above, note 23.

14. 27. The extant synopsis of William Baldwin's lost play of *Love and Life* (Feuillerat, *Edward and Mary*, 215), written for acting by the gentlemen of all the Inns of Court, lists in error "Lyfe a tabernacle" among the sixty-three characters: it was evidently the goal of the hero's pilgrimage. During the period 1546–68, there was a Temple of Venus ("*phanum veneris*") among the theatrical properties of Queens' College, Cambridge (G. C. M. Smith, Malone Society's *Collections*, II, ii. 197).

15. 28. G. R. Kernodle, *From Art to Theatre*, 133–4.

15. 29. Chambers, *E.S.*, IV, 30, gives details of this conjecture.

15. 30. The speeches of Experience are wrongly given to Science, both in the original edition and in Hazlitt's *Dodsley*, II. This is clearly wrong, as Wit and Science do not meet until IV. i, and as Will's derogatory speeches are rightly taken by Reason as referring to his wife Experience and not to his daughter Science.

15. 31. Part of this scene has been misplaced in the original and in Hazlitt's *Dodsley*, appearing in C. iii (instead of in D. i, *v*.), where the discussion concerns a visit to Science, not a fight with Tediousness.

16. 32. Hazlitt's *Dodsley*, II, 388, spoils this situation by adding a spurious "Exit" to this speech.

16. 33. See Chambers, *E.S.*, IV, 26, and Hillebrand, *The Child Actors*, 129–31, for discussion of the date and identity of the play.

17. 34. Though the epilogue is given to Virtue, I think it really belongs to Fortune. It was she, not Virtue, who

sate in place,
Presenting shew of chiefest dignitie,

and for Fortune to bow to Elizabeth makes better sense than for Virtue to do so.

17. 35. Chambers, *E.S.*, III, 35, note 1, suggests that *The Cobbler's Prophecy* requires not only this wood but also "houses" representing Raph's house, the three courts of Mars, Venus, and the Duke, and the cabin of Contempt. I think it unlikely that each, or indeed any, of these was represented by a "house," for the following reasons:

(*i*) The detailed descriptions are more likely to be substitutes for realism than accessories to it. (Venus' court, for instance, is not only "adowne the hill" from that of Mars, but the way is as smooth as glass and all the doors are of feathers, *ll.* 776–80.)

(*ii*) Characters never go directly from place to place as they do in *The Marriage of Wit and Science* or *Liberality and Prodigality*; instead they have exits marked, followed by a marked entry when they next appear at their journey's end. This is the method which I have indicated in *Mary Magdalene*, above (The Muses, for example, bid the Soldier "walk hence a flight shoot vp the hill" to Mars's "castle wall";

the Soldier "Exit," and reappears later with Mars's porter: *ll.* 578–81, 734. All the characters walk on and off in this way).

(*iii*) Characters do not point to buildings as they do in other plays (to Science's house or to Fortune's palace), though the Muses indicate "this wood" (*l.* 525). It is true that at the end a Priest remarks "The Cabbin of Contempt doth burne with fire" (*l.* 1580), but the accompanying stage-directions are vague. They certainly do not suggest that a "house" was burned, or even feigned to be burned. "Enter the Duke, his daughter, Priest, and Scholler: then compasse the stage, from one part let a smoke arise: at which place they all stay"; and, after praying, "They all rise and cast incense into the fire." The burning cabin is symbolized rather than represented (perhaps some long-burning firework was used). Only one scene, and that a discussion without action, takes place with Contempt presiding; and it is not stated to be in his cabin, though chairs seem to be provided, since the disputants are invited to "sit downe" (*l.* 255). At the end of the scene everyone, Contempt included, has a marked exit.

I suggest therefore the following setting. There is a raised platform serving as "stage" (see above, p. 10). One side of this platform represents (perhaps visually) a wood. The other side remains bare (apart from movable properties like chairs) and serves variously and successively for a place outside Raph's house, a place where Contempt presides, a place near Charon's ferry, the outside of Mars's court, the inside of Venus' court, the outside of the Duke's court, and so forth. Most of these places make only a single appearance in the action, they serve no theatrical purpose, and accordingly there is no reason to believe that they were realistically represented.

18. 36. In the First Quarto (1600), however, which Sir Walter Greg believes to have been printed from the author's manuscript (*The Editorial Problem in Shakespeare*, 2nd edn., 1951, 125), the speech is given to "Sno."; this is altered in the later and less authoritative texts of the Second Quarto ("1600," really 1619) and the First Folio (1623) to the ambiguous "Sn.". The speech is usually given to Snout in modern editions. But it is perhaps relevant that Snug, as lion, has just been brought to the audience's notice.

18. 37. To those already mentioned there should be added Edwards' *Damon and Pithias*, where a "house" representing the court is wanted (Chambers, *E.S.*, III, 32). The prologue draws attention to Dionysius' palace, and during the play characters frequently go "hence to the courte."

19. 38. Hence the vagueness of many stage-directions, particularly about stage-*effects*, *e.g.* in *All for Money* and *The Cobbler's Prophecy* (see above, notes 14 and 35). The author would not always know where, if at all, his play would be acted; for the court was selective and there was an audition to be overcome before a play was chosen. Also, if the author wrote for his own group of amateurs or professionals, he might still wish to publish the play. Some plays may have been twice performed, and undergone appropriate revision, before printing.

Horestes, which is probably the court play of 1567–8 and yet ends with a prayer in which the Lord Mayor is conspicuous, is perhaps a case in point.

19. 39. Chambers, *E.S.*, III, 23–4.

20. 40. Pollard (*The Macro Plays*, xv) and Adams (*Chief Pre-Shakespearian Dramas*, 304) see it as an inn-yard play. There is, however, the difficulty that at *l.* 554 Mankind says "I wyll in-to thi yerde, souerens, and cum a-geyn sone"; Pollard here supposes that a stable-yard was meant and that the play took place in the courtyard. There are also frequent demands for "room" (*e.g.*, at *ll.* 324, 467, 605, 624, 689, 694), which a normal inn-yard performance might not necessitate, and which hint that the play was inside the inn, with the audience impeding the doors.

21. 41. Chambers, *E.S.*, III, 35. Similarly, at the beginning of *Wealth and Health* (a Marian court play), Wealth affects discontent because he is not given a satisfactory welcome:

> No wordes I harde, nor yet no talking,
> No instrument went nor ballattes synging.
> What ayles you all thus to syt dreaming?
> Of whom take ye care?

21. 42. *Susanna*, *l.* 232. *Gammer Gurton's Needle*, II. iv, 2. For *The Marriage of Wit and Science*, see above, p. 15.

22. 43. *E.g.*, *New Custom*, *The Tide tarrieth no Man* (worshipful audience), *Youth* (all this presence), *Mundus et Infans* (seemly sirs), *Mankind*, *Impatient Poverty*, *Hickscorner* (sovereigns).

22. 44. The final prayer for Elizabeth in *Wealth and Health* may be dismissed as a publisher's addition. For details of the address to Mary immediately preceding it, see my article in *R.E.S.*, 1953, "The Political Interpretation of Two Tudor Interludes," 104–5.

22. 45. I suspect that the superfluous epilogue and the prologue to *Jack Juggler* come from another hand than that which produced the play.
References in the text to evening performances are more frequent in the first half of the sixteenth century than the second: *e.g.* *Nature* (Part I), ("Wherfore I haue ordeyned the / thys nyght to appere") *Thersites* ("If there be any present here thys nyghte" *The Weather* (Little Dick has heard that Jupiter has descended from Heaven "This night to suppe here wyth my lord," and there is a further reference to "this nyght" a little later); *Magnificence* (*l.* 365, "I had not ben here with you this nyght").

24. 46. In place of the hearty coarseness of some of Heywood's jokes, the plays written for Elizabeth's court employ a discreet form of innuendo. Thus Dandelyne, the hostess in *Liberality and Prodigality*, says of her approaching entertainment of Prodigality

> And therefore alreadie it is *definitum*,
> The Gentleman shall want nothing may please his
> *appetitum*.

And because most meates vnsawced, are motiues
to drouth,
He shall haue a Lemman to moysten his mouth,
A Lymon I meane, no Lemman I trow:
Take heed, my faire maides, you take me not so:
For though I goe not as graue as my Grandmother
Yet I haue honestie as well as another.

(*ll.* 531–8).

24. 47. *Gammer Gurton's Needle*, II. iv, 2:

DICCON: Now this gere must forward goe, for here my gammer
commeth,
Be still a while & say nothing, make here a litle romth.

For *The Marriage of Wit and Science*, see above, p. 15. In *Damon and Pithias*, Pithias is advised by the good courtier Aristippus "The kyng is at hand, stande close in the prease"; the entry of Damon is from the court. It is possible, of course, that as a stage army was engaged in *Horestes*, a stage crowd might be engaged in this play.

26. 48. *Fulgens and Lucrece*, *l.* 56.

CHAPTER II

28. 1. W. J. Lawrence, "The Practice of Doubling and its Influence on Early Dramaturgy," *Pre-Restoration Stage Studies*, 43–4. Lawrence notes that, when Henry VIII added another company to his father's professionals, the two companies were not combined into one. Feuillerat, *Edward and Mary*, 86, prints a document showing that the royal company numbered five on 5 January 1551–52. Baskervill, *The Elizabethan Jig*, 44, mentions a company of six or seven ("Sir Francis Lake's Men") playing "in the north parts" in 1556.

28. 2. Chambers, *E.S.*, II, 25.

28. 3. Chambers, *E.S.*, II, 12 note 6.

28. 4. P. Reyher, *Les Masques Anglais*, 83. Chambers, *M.S.*, II, 118.

28. 5. Chambers, *E.S.*, II, 13.

29. 6. F. S. Boas, *University Drama in the Tudor Age*, 20, 70.

29. 7. Chambers, *E.S.*, III, 179.

29. 8. For the inadequacy of the doubling, see the Malone Society's edition of the play (McKerrow and Greg), xiii–xiv.

30. 9. See my article "The Political Interpretation of Two Tudor Interludes," *R.E.S.*, 1953, 102–108.

30. 10. Lawrence, 55.

31. 11. Chambers, *E.S.*, III, 351. The dialogue source of the play is the *Juvenis, Pater, Uxor* of Ravisius Textor: see F. Holthausen in *Englische Studien*, XXI, 1902.

31. 12. Erasmus, *Colloquies* (N. Bailey's translation, 1733), 183. More, *Works* (1553), 404: Tyndale "preacheth lyke a player in a fond enterlude, and playeth sometime the frere, sometime the foxe, sometime the foole, and sometime the outeright ribauld."

31. 13, Ramsay (intro. to Skelton's *Magnificence*, E.E.T.S., cxxxii) so divides *Wisdom* (five actors and six mutes), *Nature* (six actors), *Hickscorner* (four), *Mundus et Infans* (two), *Magnificence* (five), and the incomplete *The Four Elements* (five).

32. 14. J. W. Harris, *John Bale*, 100–3; *King John* (Malone Society), xvii–xviii.

32. 15. Lawrence, 52. See also Chambers, *M.S.*, II, 188.

32. 16. Lawrence, 52. Harris, 105, says that it is possible to divide the "nineteen" parts among nine actors.

33. 17. The text of *King John* is fully discussed in the Malone Society's edition of the play, and I accept the editors' general conclusions, xxii–xxiii. (Bale wrote a two-part play before 1536, and re-cast it in one part—the A-text of the MS.—in 1538 for performance by Cromwell's Men at Cranmer's house. Under Edward VI he revised not this but his original two-part play again. In 1561 he revised the A-text, incorporating especially in the second part much of the Edwardian recension, and dividing it again into two. The latter portion of the MS.—the B-text—is entirely in Bale's hand and completes the 1561 version.)

The doubling in the A-text is impracticable at times: *e.g.*, Sedition at first doubles with Civil Order (*ll.* 314, 548), but later they appear together (*ll.* 1196–1276), and at this point there is no indication that another actor has been brought in.

Though I have distributed the characters according to the action of the whole revised version of 1561, I have followed, where practicable, the doubling of the A-text: thus England doubles with Clergy (*ll.* 154, 1488) but not with Dissimulation (*l.* *59 in the cancelled part of the A-text); Private Wealth doubles with Nobility (*ll.* 616, 1062, 1394, 1532, and *80 in the cancelled portion of the A-text); and Civil Order doubles with Commonalty (*l.* 1488) but not with Sedition (*ll.* 314, 548).

The Interpreter's speech creates an artificial act-division in the play. Really the action continues, and has not been revised to allow for the Interpreter's presence:

> The Pope sends out Pandulphus to interdict King John's land, bids Stephen Langton cause the bishops to curse John, and orders Raymundus to raise foreign wars against him. Pandulphus (Private Wealth) has the direction "here go owt & dresse for nobylyte" (1062) but the others have no marked exits and I think remain to hear the Pope announce that he will call a general council to promote the cause of Rome, which "wyll be to vs, a perpetuall furderaunce." After this speech, which does not read to me like a soliloquy, comes the direction "here the pope go owt & dyssymvlacyon & nobylyte cum in & say" (speech follows). The Malone editors say that in this direction "dyssymvlacyon" is an error for "sedycyon": but I think the verb is plural and that the Pope and Dissimulation are to go out here, leaving on stage Sedition, who replies to Nobility's speech and has no entry marked.

33. 18. L. M. Oliver, "William Wager and *The Trial of Treasure*," *H.L.Q.*, August 1946.

34. 19. The doubling recommended on the title-page (see Chapter II, p. 40) could be left unchanged for actors 1, 2, 5, and 6, and the other parts re-distributed as follows: 3—Contentation, Servant, Prophet; 4—Temerity, Satan, Rest; 7—Inconsideration, Enough, Hireling, Ignorance.

35. 20. The passages are quoted in my article, "Some Notes on Thomas Lupton's *All for Money*," *N. & Q.*, June 1954.

36. 21. Lawrence, 52.

37. 22. Willard Farnham, *The Medieval Heritage of Elizabethan Tragedy*, 243. He finds the play "lacking in dramatic cohesion," 245.

38. 23. "Quasse" is intentional and not an error for "quaffe" (see examples in *O.E.D.*: the meaning is to eat or drink heartily).

The treatment of these entrances and exits in Hazlitt's *Dodsley*, III, is thoroughly confused and incorrect.

41. 24. Sharp, *Coventry Mysteries*, 38: in the Coventry play *The Destruction of Jerusalem* (1584) one man plays "Ananus" and another "a pece of Ananus" ; a third plays "Mathias and Esron," but a fourth also plays "Esron his parte."

42. 25. *Epitaph on Sal[omon] Pavy a Child of Queen Elizabeths Chappel* (Epigrammes, 1616, cxx).

43. 26. See above, p. 15. It would be natural to call the play after its two most memorable characters: compare *Much Ado about Nothing*, called *Benedicte and Betteris* when given at court in 1613 (see E. K. Chambers, *William Shakespeare*, II, 343).

45. 27. "Getteth"="jetteth": "here"="hair": "warbelith"="wobbleth, waddleth."

45. 28. In his *Susanna*, Thomas Garter confesses that "we cannot bewtify the same with musickes song." I cannot guess why this was impossible. The play seems to contain parts for boys (Susanna and her two maids), and the parts are distributed among eight actors (though not, apparently, by the author: for the vice and the crier are listed as doubled with each other, whereas the crier is the temporary employment of the vice).

45. 29. *New Custom*: the song is not given in full, or even called by a title.

46. 30. I wish to record here my gratitude to Dr J. E. Stevens for several stimulating conversations about music and the court drama.

48. 31. Chambers, *E.S.*, II, 12 note 6.

CHAPTER III

50. 1. Jonson complained of those masque-devisers who so

> Attire the persons as no thought can teach
> Sense what they are . . .

(*Expostulation with Inigo Jones*, quoted by Reyher, *Les Masques Anglais*, 392. Reyher's account of the costumes in Tudor masques and disguisings is excellent.)

50. 2. For the costume of God in miracles, see Cohen, *La mise en scène dans le théâtre religieux français*, 223, and *cf.* Rabelais, *Pantagruel*, IV. xiii.

51. 3. *Wily Beguiled* (Malone Society Reprints, 1912), *ll.* 1037–8. The devil is in feathers in the *Chester Plays* (E.E.T.S.), 6; in the Coventry miracles he was variously dressed in leather or in canvas covered with horsehair (Sharp, *Coventry Mysteries*, 57). For animal-headed devils see Nicoll, *Development of the Theatre*, 75, and figs. 60, 63. For a French fifteenth-century devil in a bear-skin covered with fireworks see Cohen, 95. The quotation from More is from his *Works* (1557), 414. Cushman's suggestion (*The Devil and the Vice*, 49) that Satan in *Lusty Juventus* is dressed as a swine, because Hypocrisy mistakes his voice for "a sowes groning," is fanciful. For the devil's snout in the Newcastle *Noah*, see Waterhouse, *Non-Cycle Mystery Plays* (E.E.T.S.), xlii.

51. 4. *The Jew of Malta*, Act III. A scene or two later, Ithamore pointedly presents his master with a ladle, as the "long spoon" necessary when one sups with the devil. In *The Merchant of Venice* Shylock is explicitly described by his servant as "a kinde of diuell" and "the very diuell incarnation" (II. ii), and this monologue depends for much of its comedy on the morality reminiscences, as Lancelot Gobbo hearkens alternately to the advice of his conscience and to that of the fiend.

52. 5. The point that Despair and Mischief in *Magnificence* are devils is made by Ramsay in his introduction to the E.E.T.S. edition, clxx. The German version of the lost English play is re-translated and printed by R. Simpson, *The School of Shakespeare*, II: in Act V, when the Prodigal is wretched, "Enter Satan with a drawn sword," and Satan says "My name's Despair"; his subsequent speeches are headed Despair, but when Hope expels him it is with the words "Hence, straightway, Satan," 114.

52. 6. The British Museum copy (C. 34 e. 14) of *The longer thou livest, the more Fool thou art* has a MS. note opposite the name of Confusion in "The Players names," reading "the devilles messenger." The note is in a hand of the late sixteenth century and is probably contemporary with the publication of the play. The name Confusion is given to a devil in R. Robinson, *The Rewarde of Wickednesse* (1574), B iii, *v*.

53. 7. Lupton also writes, in his *A Dreame of the Deuill and Diues* (1615 edn.), F vii, *v*., that those who dress extravagantly on earth will at Doomsday "weare the terrible and dreadfull garmentes of Gods curse, imbrodered with the vnquenchable flames of hell fire." For the souls at Coventry see Sharp, *Coventry Mysteries*, 68.

53. 8. Lawrence has suggested (*Pre-Restoration Stage Studies*, 55) that vizards were in general use and were the means whereby actors doubling several parts were able to differentiate between the characters. But there is no evidence for this, though there are recorded masks worn by tyrants and devils in miracle-plays (Sharp, *Coventry Mysteries*, 28; Craig, *Two Coventry Corpus Christi Plays*, 94) and by various participants in disguisings at court (see Feuillerat, *Edward and Mary* and *Elizabeth*, indexes under "masks" and "vizards"). For the disguising of 1515 see Hall's *Chronicle*, 580; and *cf.* Feuillerat, *Elizabeth*, 200, and Spenser, *Faerie Queene*, I. 7. viii (the savage giant Orgoglio). For illustrations of "wild men" see R. van Marle, *Iconographie*, I, 190–2. For devils with clubs see Sharp, 31 ("a stafe for the demon" at Coventry in 1567); Craig, 94 ("the giandes head and clubbe"); and Chambers, *M.S.*, I, 209 note 3, 214.

53. 9. For the angel's costume at Queens' College, Cambridge, see G. C. M. Smith, Malone Society's *Collections* II, ii, 197. Chastitie in Lyndsay's play is "cled in quhyte" and "lyk ane Angell," and Divyne Correctioun has "wantoun wings" (*ll.* 1304, 1415, 1670).

54. 10. See Latimer, *Sermons*, 126. For the masque of 1573 see Feuillerat, *Elizabeth*, 206, and for the 1527 play see R. Gibson's contemporary account printed by Collier, *H.E.D.P.*, I, 107–8.

54. 11. See Lyly, *Sapho and Phao*, III. iv. A detailed account of the origin and use of the woodcuts on Tudor title-pages is given by McKerrow in his introduction to *Youth* (Bang's *Materialen*, XII), xvi–xx. For Stephen Batman see *D.N.B.*

54. 12. Feuillerat, *Edward and Mary*, 3 (and note); *Elizabeth*, 193.

55. 13. See below, p. 80.

56. 14. *New Custom*, however, demands special mention because of another visible contrast, namely that between youth and age. The play's moral lesson is the paradoxical one that the "new" ways of worship are in fact older than the long-established ones. Accordingly Perverse Doctrine is "an olde Popishe priest" and Ignorance "another, but elder," whereas their opponent New Custom ("a Minister") is much younger in appearance; but, as the prologue states, "All thinges be not soe as in sight they doe seeme," and New Custom's declaration of his real age provides the most dramatic moment of a largely undramatic play:

> P.D.: Whie, how olde art thou, tell mee I pray thee hartely?
> N.C.: Elder then you I perceiue.
> P.D.: What older than I?
> The younge knaue by the masse not fully thirtie,
> Woulde be elder then I, that am aboue sixtie?
> N.C.: A thousande, and a halfe, that surely is my age.

For the lost play of 1527, see note 10 to this chapter.

57. 15. Lyndsay, *Works* (ed. Hamer), II, 4.

57. 16. For R. Willis's eye-witness account of *The Cradle of Security* (in *Mount Tabor*, 1639) see Collier, *H.E.D.P.*, II, 196. The play was probably acted between 1565 and 1575 (Harbage, *Annals*).

57. 17. *Hamlet*, IV. vii. (The passage does not appear in the Folio.)

57. 18. Jonson, *The Alchemist*, IV. vii.

58. 19. The proverb has a prophetic force: for later Lust and Treasure are turned to dust and rust.

60. 20. Compare *The Cobbler's Prophecy*, where Charon complains of his toil in ferrying covetous misers:

> I thinke they bring their money to hell,
> For they way the diuel and al.

60. 21. Feuillerat, *Elizabeth*, 244: "skynnes to furr the hoode in sabastians playe" (1 February 1574–75). H. N. Hillebrand, *The Child Actors*, 129–31, identifies the play as *Liberality and Prodigality* and the author as Sebastian Westcott, I think convincingly. For the use of fur to clothe the usurer, see C. T. Wright, "Some Conventions regarding the Usurer in Elizabethan Literature," *S.P.*, XXXI (1934), 189–91.

60. 22. Autolycus in *The Winter's Tale*, IV. iii.

61. 23. See below, p. 75.

63. 24. Feuillerat, *Elizabeth*, 244, 246, 234. (Compare Pecunia's costume in Plate XI.) For the probability that the costume was intended for a performance of *Liberality and Prodigality* see H. N. Hillebrand, *The Child Actors*, 129–31, and note 21 to this chapter.

63. 25. My point about Fluellen's prolixity is reinforced by Fortune's first speech in *The longer thou livest, the more Fool thou art*, where it is assumed that the audience can recognize Fortune on sight; she calls for homage because she rules all worldly matters, and then says that she will exalt Moros in order to be revenged on mankind (the audience) for their neglect of her. It is only in the last four lines of her speech that she names herself:

> By that you shall learne I trowe,
> To do your dutie to a lady so hye,
> He shall teach you fortune to knowe,
> And to honour hyr till you die.

64. 26. R. van Marle, *Iconographie*, 199, fig. 224 (a German woodcut of 1545). Other double-faced Fortunes are in a woodcut to Boccaccio's *De Casibus Virorum Illustrium* (Brugge, 1483) and in drawings in MSS at Balliol College, Oxford (MS. 238, fol. 123 r), and at the Vatican (Cod. Pal. Lat. 1066). Photographs of the last three examples are at the Warburg Institute.

64. 27. Time appeared in Elizabeth's coronation pageant at London (Nichols, *Progresses Eliz.*, I, 49 ff.), with his usual attributes.

64. 28. Nichols, *Progresses Eliz.*, I, 50. For the lost Edwardian interlude see Feuillerat, *Edward and Mary*, 245.

65. 29. Furies had appeared in 1551–52 (Feuillerat, *Edward and Mary*, 73, "vj mouldes for serpentes for the same hedpeces"). See also the first dumb-show in *The Misfortunes of Arthur* (1587–8), *Dodsley*, IV, 251.

66. 30. Feuillerat, *Edward and Mary*, 142, 262.

66. 31. See Chaucer, *House of Fame*, III, 1365–92. For the 1518 disguising see Hall's *Chronicle*, 595, and Reyher, *Les Masques Anglais*, 399–400. The opening direction of *2 Henry IV* is found in the Quarto, not the Folio.

66. 32. Feuillerat, *Edward and Mary*, 245.

66. 33. Feuillerat, *Elizabeth*, 241. For the identification of the play see note 21 to this chapter.

67. 34. Bale's *King John*, *ll.* 718–27.

68. 35. See L. Hotson, *Shakespeare's Motley*, 33–43; Dekker, *Satiromastix*, V. ii.

68. 36. Printed by Nichols, *Progresses James*, I, 16.

68. 37. For the parasite's costume at Jesus College, Cambridge, see G. C. M. Smith, Malone Society's *Collections*, II, ii, 212. Bradbrook, *Themes and Conventions*, 15, gives references to the parasite's costume (descriptions not extant). In the eighteenth-century dramatic satire on Walpole's administration *The Golden Rump*, a troop of time-servers and place-seekers wear "party-colour'd Robes of Black and White," which may be a late survival of this same tradition (*Gentleman's Magazine*, 1737, 168). The moral significance of black and white in a single costume, which is obvious, is stated by Stephen Batman, *The Golden Booke of the Leaden Goddes* (1577), fol. 4:

> Mercurie was porctraited with winges at head and feete, wearing an Hat of white & blacke colloures . . . By Mercurie Marchauntes be ment . . . the whyte & blacke coloured Hat, signifieth their subtilty, which for greedines of gaine, spare not to face white for blacke, & blacke for white.

68. 38. The costumes have not only been brought up to date, but made more extravagant than those in Breu's woodcut. Note particularly the added feather in the hats of Acolastus and Pamphagus: this was a distinguishing feature of the stage prodigal; see above, pp. 57–58.

70. 39. Hamer, while he is cautious about Falset and Dissait, maintains that Flatterie is dressed as a fool and that his unfrocking is like the clergy's, and that this use of "the *sottie* element" characterizes and links both parts of the play (Lyndsay's *Works*, IV, 152, 157–60).

70. 40. Hamer thinks (IV, 157) that Flatterie has "come on a ship of fools" on the strength of his account of a voyage, and points out that Dissait's opening line is "Stand by the gait that I may steir." But in *Hickscorner* (where there is no reason for supposing that the three revellers are dressed as fools) Hickscorner shouts before his first entry

> Ale the helme ale vere shot of vere sayle vera,

and Freewill's comment is

> Cockes body herke he is in a shyppe on the see.

The idea may perhaps be connected with that of the Ship of Fools, but in these plays it seems merely a way of introducing a noisy and irresponsible character. Such disreputable and absurd tricks are common to comic characters, but this in itself is not enough to establish that they are wearing the professional fool's garb.

71. 41. Jonson, *The Devil is an Ass*, I. i.

71. 42. See previous reference; and Shakespeare, *Twelfth Night*, IV. ii.

71. 43. Thus Moros, in *The longer thou livest, the more Fool thou art*, handles his sword absurdly, but he is not the vice; nor is he dressed in a fool's coat, since his investiture with one is the climax of the play.

71. 44. Skelton, *The Bowge of Court*, *ll.* 344–58.

CHAPTER IV

73. 1. Tyndale, *Works* (1573), I, 60 (*The Wicked Mammon*, 1528). Compare Bale's interlude *John Baptist's Preaching in the Wilderness*, where the Pharisee and Sadducee complain that "thys fellawe preacheth newe lernynge" and hope that "with a lytle helpe, of an heretyke he wyll smell"; the epilogue warns the audience against the "vayne fantasyes" and inventions of the Pope, which are meant when the prophet denounces the Pharisee's corruption of scripture for personal profit, and the Sadducee's belief that salvation can be purchased by outward works.

In his *King John*, Bale has modelled the speeches of Verity (in the final scene) on Tyndale's *The Obedience of a Christian Man*: see H. McCusker, *John Bale*, 90–3.

74. 2. Tyndale, *Works*, I, 184.

74. 3. Tyndale, *Works*, I, 184. (*An Exposition, etc.*)

74. 4. Tyndale, *Works*, I, 129, 143 (*The Obedience of a Christian Man*). Compare William Roy and Jerome Barlow, *Rede me and be not wrothe* (1528), ed. E. Arber (1871), 46, where it is said of the Gospel

> By my trothe they sett hym a fyre
> Openly in London cite.

75. 5. For *The Whore of Babylon*, see above, pp. 64–65. For the other plays, see below, pp. 76–77.

75. 6. Bale uses the theme of blindness again in *King John*, where England brings in her son Commonalty, who is poor and blind. His poverty is due to the clergy's rapacity, the blindness to "want of knowlage, in christes lyuely veryte." The blindness can be cured if the truth is taught; as England explains,

> his outward blyndnes, ys but a sygnyficacyon
> of blyndnes in sowle, for lacke of informacyon
> in the word of god . . .

78. 7. *Julius Caesar*, II. i. *Fair Em*, II. 1. Compare the Earl of Northumberland's discarding of his "nice crutch" and "sickly Quoife" in *2 Henry IV*, I. i.

78. 8. Hall's *Chronicle*, 597 (court disguising of 7 March 1519). Spectacle and change of character combine in an Italian morisco given in 1521 before Pope Leo X, where hermits are turned into lovers by Cupid's arrows: "they threw off their religious habits and showed themselves to be gallant gentlemen, ready to fall upon each other in a frenzy of courage and jealousy" (E. Welsford, *The Court Masque*, 90).

78. 9. A good example is Shakespeare's dramatization, in *Henry VIII*, I. iv, of an incident related by Holinshed.

79. 10. See *2 Henry VI*, II. iv., and *The Duchess of Malfi*, IV. i. For the incident in *Impatient Poverty* see below, p. 86. A similar incident takes place in the French fifteenth-century *moralité* of *Bien-Avisé, Mal-Avisé*: Humilité gives Bien-Avisé a robe of hers to replace his fine clothes before he can go to Confession and Pénitence (E. Lintilhac, *La Comédie, Moyen Age et Renaissance*, 115).

80. 11. Copland's edition is printed directly from Waley's. The pagination is similar and so are the abbreviated names of the speakers. It is therefore clear that he is responsible for the substitution of "bokes" for Waley's "bedes."

81. 12. Hypocrisy derisively salutes him as "maister doctor" and "gentle syr Iohn" on account of his religious conversation, and asks to see his "portus" (properly a breviary, but here a Bible); Juventus is carrying this, since he refuses to show it to Hypocrisy and maintains that it is not a book to jest upon.

82. 13. Hypocrisy (C. i, *v.*) exhorts the papists to wear

> Square cappes, longe gownes, with tippettes of silke,
> Braue coopes in the churche, surplices as white as milke,
> Beades and suchelike, all these beare the price.

82. 14. Chambers, *E.S.*, IV, 37, who does not offer his own opinion, mentions Fleay's suggestion to this effect.

82. 15. L. M. Oliver, "John Foxe and the drama *New Custom*," *H.L.Q.* August 1947. The story of a Roman Catholic who betrayed his Protestant brother in order to gain the family estate, quoted by Avarice in *New Custom*, first appears in the 1570 edition of Foxe.

82. 16. The play proceeds by argumentative statement and rejoinder. The sole literary influence, which is strong, is that of Udall: it appears in the *enjambement* of the prologue, and the equally characteristic line-by-line repartee of some of the dialogue. Udall's influence may not have reached the author of *New Custom* early, however, for the play shows no intimacy with the usual dramatic techniques of this period; like *The Conflict of Conscience*, it is a stolid work and lacks dramatic animation.

82. 17. *ll.* 627. It is not stated that he changes into another costume on entering the Castle of Perseverance, but he may perhaps do so nevertheless; his later change, in old age, into "a sloppe" (*l.* 2489), is not indicated in the directions.

83. 18. The character must at first wear only some light clothing: *cf. The Castle of Perseverance*, where Humanum Genus calls himself "nakyd" but shortly afterwards says "bare & pore is my clothynge" (*ll.* 279, 293).

84. 19. See above, p. 60.

85. 20. Lyndsay, *Works*, II: *Ane Satyre*, *ll.* 3723–30).

85. 21. But compare also the black-faced fool of the morris dances (see Chambers, *M.S.*, I, 199 note 4, 214).

87. 22. The disguising of the vices in the interludes lies (I think) behind an image in *The Merchant of Venice* (III. ii.):

> There is no vice so simple, but assumes
> Some marke of vertue on his outward parts.

("vice" is the reading of the second and later Folios for the "voice" of the Quartos and First Folio.)

88. 23. *Ludus Coventriae* (ed. Block), 225–9.

89. 24. Bale, *King John*, *ll.* 934–43. See above, p. 67.

90. 25. W. J. Lawrence, "The Practice of Doubling" in *Pre-Restoration Stage Studies*, 53–4.

90. 26. Though the play employs the basic plot of Redford's *Wit and Science* and the anonymous *The Marriage of Wit and Science*, it is itself no more than a piece of frivolous entertainment centred upon the vice's part. Its allegory is illogical, no attempt is made to define "honest recreation," and Irksomeness (the adversary of Wit) is dead by the end of Act I. The epilogue, with its request that the audience will mark the moral, is pure impudence. The farce itself is of a pedestrian nature, and is largely plagiarized from *Cambises* (*e.g.* in I. iii) and *Gammer Gurton's Needle* (*e.g.* in II. iii, II. iv).

91. 27. *l.* 104; *cf. ll.* 420–1, 476.

91. 28. *l.* 1585. The word "gallant" had acquired by *c.* 1550 a derogatory sense largely independent of its social implications: *e.g.*, in the ballad of *Little John Nobody* (Percy's *Reliques*, II, 7) the Reformers are called "these gay gallants, that wil construe the gospel"; and in *Three Lords and Three Ladies of London* the four knaves Fraud, Dissimulation, Usury, and Simony are called "gallants" in the *dramatis personae*, though in *Three Ladies of London* (and presumably in this play too) each wore a distinctive dress, see above, pp. 62, 67.

92. 29. A list of players' costumes, for the non-return of which John Rastell the dramatist sued Henry Walton in 1530, includes "a player's garment of green, lined with red tuke and with Roman letters stitched upon it, of blue and red sarcenet" (Pollard, *Fifteenth-Century Prose and Verse*, 305–21, prints the whole document). At an Augsburg political dumb-show of 1530 the characters' names—Reuchlin, Erasmus, Luther, the Emperor, the Pope—were written on their backs (J. A. Froude, *Life and Letters of Erasmus*, 390), while in Elizabeth's coronation-pageants Truth wore hers on her breast (Nichols, *Progresses Elizabeth*, I, 50).

CHAPTER V

95. 1. Dürer, in the series *Klassiker der Kunst* ed. Friedrich Winkler, Vol. IV, 373. The virtues are set in the stocks while a false judge or ruler sits enthroned, with Piety asleep in a cradle before him. Flettner's large engraving, of which I reproduce a detail, is shown in full in Max Geisberg, *Der Deutsche Einblatt-Holzschnitt*, No. 813; a full account of the original, and of later copies, is given by Campbell Dodgson, *Catalogue of Early German and Flemish Woodcuts, British Museum*, I, 358.

96. 2. W. J. Lawrence, *Pre-Restoration Stage Studies*, 253.

96. 3. In the first part of *Tamburlaine* (*ll.* 369–72). The entry in his chariot is in the second part, *l.* 4175.

96. 4. Hazlitt's *Dodsley*, VIII, 369.

98. 5. This direction (*l.* 758) was, as the Malone Society editors note, added by the scribe in revision, in a space which he had originally left blank.

99. 6. "Wrestle, and let Lust seem to haue the better at first": "Staye and then speake": "Caste him, and let him arise again." These directions show that the fight was a carefully-planned one.

107. 7. Worldly Man, when he awakens, tells Covetous

> And me thought before me the plague of God did stand:
> Redy to strike me with a Sworde in his hand.

Similarly, the denunciation of Lust by God's Visitation in *The Trial of Treasure*—

> Thou insipient foole that hast folowed thy luste—

is apostrophe, for Lust is unaware of his presence and continues to dally with Treasure and Pleasure: it is an effective scene. With the direction in *Enough is as good as a Feast* compare "Dispayre enter in some ougly shape, and stand behind him" in *The Tide tarrieth no Man* (the temptation of Wastefulness to suicide). This formal positioning of the characters is meant to show that the happenings are taking place at a spiritual, not a physical, level.

108. 8. The text has, in error,

> WORLDLY MAN: Of, of, of, of, what more?

I have restored the prefix to Ignorance's speech.

111. 9. The full title—*The Contention between Liberality and Prodigality*—is misleading. There are two pairs of rivals in the play: Fortune and Virtue on the allegorical plane, Prodigality and Tenacity (who are human type-characters) on the literal plane. Liberality, who is Virtue's steward, is balanced in the play's scheme against Vanity, who is Fortune's.

112. 10. The conflict of Virtue and Fortune, though it is nominally the theme of the play, is never brought to an issue, though one is forecast by both Fortune and Liberality (*ll.* 275–84, 318–19). Towards the end of the play, Money is committed to Virtue's care by the Sheriff (who has no allegorical function, merely the literal one of pursuing and arresting Prodigality): "Then, Madam, I pray you appoint some Officer to take the money," *l.* 1176.

116. 11. When Money is finally committed to his charge, Liberality says

> First, from thy bands Ile set thee free,
> And after, thy sickenes cured shall be.
>
> (*ll.* 1197–8).

118. 12. Dr M. C. Bradbrook has kindly drawn my attention to the end of Dekker's *Old Fortunatus*, where Elizabeth is made the judge between Fortune, Vice, and Virtue. Vice flees, and Fortune declares herself submissive to the Queen, whom Virtue lauds as a "sacred deitie."

DATES OF THE PRINCIPAL PLAYS DISCUSSED

(including all extant Tudor interludes)

THE dating of the great majority of Tudor interludes is a matter of conjecture, and accordingly the following chronological table is put forward as a convenient guide to the dates of composition which I have accepted or arrived at in this study. For further detailed discussion of dates of composition the reader is referred to E. K. Chambers, *The Elizabethan Stage* (1923), and to *The Year's Work in English Studies* for works published later than Chambers's.

Dates of original publication, where known, are given in the Bibliography.

1400–25? *The Castle of Perseverance*
1400–25? *The Pride of Life*
1450–1500? *Mankind*
1450–1500? *Wisdom*
1495? *Everyman*
1495? *Nature*
1497? *Fulgens and Lucrece*
1508? *Mundus et Infans*
1513? *Hickscorner*
1515? *Good Order*
1516? *Magnificence*
1517? *The Four Elements*
1520? *Youth*
1520? *John the Evangelist*
1521? *Witty and Witless*
1525? *Love*
1527? *The Weather*
1527? *Calisto and Melibea*
1527? *Gentleness and Nobility*
1527? *Godly Queen Hester*
1529? *The Four PP*
1529? *The Pardoner and the Friar*
1529? *Johan Johan*
1530? *The Prodigal Son*
1532? *Three Laws* (revised 1538?)
1535? *Temperance and Humility*
1535? *King John* (revised 1538? revised 1561?)
1536? *Christ's Resurrection* (*The Resurrection of Our Lord*)
1537 *Thersites*
1537? *Albion Knight*
1538 *God's Promises*
1538 *John the Baptist*
1538 *The Temptation of Our Lord*
1539? *Wit and Science*
1547? *Impatient Poverty*
1550? *Somebody, Avarice and Minister*
1550? *Love feigned and unfeigned*
1550? *Nice Wanton*
1550? *Lusty Juventus*
1550? *Jacob and Esau*
1552 *Ane Satyre of the Thrie Estaitis* (expansion of a shorter, lost, interlude of 1540)
1553 *Respublica*
1553? *Gammer Gurton's Needle*
1553? *Roister Doister*
1553? *Jack Juggler*
1554? *Wealth and Health*
1559? *Patient Grissell*
1560? *The Disobedient Child*
1560? *Tom Tyler and his Wife*
1560? *All for Money*
1560? *Apius and Virginia*
1561? *The Pedlar's Prophecy*
1564? *The longer thou livest, the more Fool thou art*
1564? *Enough is as good as a Feast*
1565? *The Cruel Debtor*
1565? *The Trial of Treasure*

1565? *King Darius*
1565 *Damon and Pithias*
1566? *Mary Magdalene*
1567 *Horestes*
1567 *The Marriage of Wit and Science*
1567? *Liberality and Prodigality*
1568? *Like will to Like*
1569? *Cambises*
1569? *Susanna*
1570? *New Custom*
1570? *Misogonus*
1572? *The Conflict of Conscience*
1575 *The Glass of Government*
1576? *The Tide tarrieth No Man*
1576? *Common Conditions*
1579? *The Marriage of Wit and Wisdom*
1581 *Three Ladies of London*
1589? *Three Lords and Three Ladies of London*
1589? *The Cobbler's Prophecy*

BIBLIOGRAPHY

Abbreviations.

C.B.E.L.	Cambridge Bibliography of English Literature.
C.H.E.L.	Cambridge History of English Literature.
D.N.B.	Dictionary of National Biography.
E.E.T.S.	Early English Text Society.
Eng. Stud.	Englische Studien.
J.E.G.P.	Journal of English and Germanic Philology.
M.L.N.	Modern Language Notes.
M.L.R.	Modern Language Review.
M.P.	Modern Philology.
N. & Q.	Notes and Queries.
P.M.L.A.	Publications of the Modern Language Association of America.
P.Q.	Philological Quarterly.
R.E.S.	Review of English Studies.
S.P.	Studies in Philology.
S.T.C.	Short Title Catalogue 1476–1640 (A. W. Pollard and G. R. Redgrave), 1946.
S.T.S.	Scottish Text Society.
T.L.S.	The Times Literary Supplement.

Collections and Series of Plays.

Hazlitt's Dodsley.	Robert Dodsley, *A Select Collection of Old Plays*, fourth edition by W. C. Hazlitt, 15 vols, 1874–76.
Brandl.	Alois Brandl, *Quellen des weltlichen Dramas in England vor Shakespeare* in *Quellen und Forschungen zur Sprach- und Culturgeschichte der germanischen Volker*, LXXX, 1898.
Shakespeare Jahrbuch.	*Jahrbuch der deutschen Shakespeare-Gesellschaft*, 1897–.
Manly.	J. M. Manly, *Specimens of Pre-Shakespearean Drama*, 2 vols, Boston, 1897–98, 1900–03.
Bang.	W. Bang (general editor), *Materialen zur Kunde des älteren englischen Dramas*, Louvain, 1902–.
Gayley.	C. M. Gayley (general editor), *Representative English Comedies*, 3 vols, New York, 1903–14.
Adams.	J. Q. Adams, *Chief Pre-Shakespearean Dramas*, Boston, 1924.
T.F.T.	Tudor Facsimile Texts, issued by J. S. Farmer, 143 vols, 1907–14.
M.S.R.	Malone Society Reprints (general editor W. W. Greg), 1907–.

Plays listed alphabetically.

This list of editions is not exhaustive. The first entry is the text which I have consulted either in an original copy or a modern facsimile. When earlier texts exist they are mentioned. The modern editions have been chosen for their accessibility, or reliability, or both.

Acolastus (Written in Latin by De Volder, also called Gnapheus; English translation by W. Palsgrave), T. Berthelet, 1540.
P. L. Carver, E.E.T.S., 1937.

Albion Knight (anonymous), T. Colwell (fragment), n.d. (1566?).
M.S.R., *Collections*, I. iii, 1909.

All for Money (T. Lupton), Roger Warde and Richard Mundee, 1578.
T.F.T., 1910.
E. Vogel, *Shakespeare Jahrbuch*, XL, 1904.

Apius and Virginia (anonymous: 'R. B.'), W. How for R. Jhones, 1575.
T.F.T., 1908.
M.S.R., 1911.
Hazlitt's Dodsley, IV.

Calisto and Melibea (anonymous: J. Rastell?), J. Rastell, n.d. (1525?).
M.S.R., 1908.
T.F.T., 1909.
Hazlitt's Dodsley, I.

Cambises (T. Preston), J. Allde, n.d. (1570?).
T.F.T., 1910.
Adams.
Hazlitt's Dodsley, IV.

The Castle of Perseverance (anonymous), MS.
F. J. Furnivall and A. W. Pollard, *The Macro Plays*, E.E.T.S., 1904.

Christ's Resurrection (anonymous: J. Bale?), MS.
M.S.R., 1912.

The Cobbler's Prophecy (R. Wilson), John Danter, 1594.
W. Dibelius, *Shakespeare Jahrbuch*, XXXIII, 1897.
T.F.T., 1911.
M.S.R., 1914.

Common Conditions (anonymous), W. How for J. Hunter, 1576.
C.F.T. Brooke, 1915.

The Conflict of Conscience (N. Woodes *or* Wood), R. Bradocke, 1581.
T.F.T., 1911.
M.S.R., 1952.
Hazlitt's Dodsley, VI.

The Cruel Debtor (W. Wager), T. Colwell (fragments), n.d. (1566?).
M.S.R., *Collections*, I. iv and v, 1911, and II. ii, 1923.

Damon and Pithias (R. Edwards), Richard Jones, 1571.
T.F.T., 1908.
Adams.
Hazlitt's Dodsley, IV.

The Disobedient Child (T. Ingelend), T. Colwell, n.d. (1570?),
T.F.T., 1908.
Hazlitt's Dodsley, II.
J. S. Farmer, *Dramatic Writings of Richard Wever and Thomas Ingelend*, 1905.

Enough is as good as a Feast (W. Wager), J. Allde, n.d. (1565?).
S. de Ricci (Huntington facsimile, New York), 1920.

Everyman (anonymous: from a Dutch source?), J. Skot, n.d. (*S.T.C.* 10606). Three other early editions.
Bang, IV, 1904.
Adams.
Hazlitt's Dodsley, I.
Numerous other editions.

The Four Elements (J. Rastell), J. Rastell (fragment), n.d. (1525?).
T.F.T., 1908.
Hazlitt's Dodsley, I.
J. S. Farmer, *Six Anonymous Plays*, 1905.

The Four PP (J. Heywood), W. Myddylton, n.d. (1545?).
T.F.T., 1908.
Hazlitt's Dodsley, I.
Manly, I.
Adams.

Fulgens and Lucrece (H. Medwall), J. Rastell, n.d. (before 1520).
S. de Ricci (Huntington facsimile, New York), 1920.
F. S. Boas and A. W. Reed, 1926.

Gammer Gurton's Needle (anonymous: 'Mr S.'; W. Stevenson?), T. Colwell, 1575.
T.F.T., 1910.
H. F. B. Brett-Smith, 1920.
Hazlitt's Dodsley, III.
Manly, II.
Gayley, I.
Adams.
Numerous other editions.

Gentleness and Nobility (anonymous: J. Rastell?), J. Rastell, n.d. (1525?).
T.F.T., 1908.
K. W. Cameron, 1941.

The Glass of Government (G. Gascoigne), H. M. for C. Barker, 1575.
J. W. Cunliffe, *The Works of George Gascoigne*, 1910.

Godly Queen Hester (anonymous), W. Pickering and T. Hacket, 1561.
Bang, V, 1904.
J. S. Farmer, *Anonymous Plays*, series 2, 1906.

God's Promises (J. Bale), D. van den Straten? Wesel? 1547?
T.F.T., 1908.
Hazlitt's Dodsley, I.

Good Order (J. Skelton), W. Rastell (fragment), 1533.
G. L. Frost and R. Nash, *S.P.*, XLI, 1944.

Hickscorner (anonymous), W. de Worde, n.d. (?1510 in *S.T.C.*, but the play probably written 1513).
T.F.T., 1908.
Hazlitt's Dodsley, I.
Manly, I.
J. S. Farmer, *Six Anonymous Plays*, 1905.

Horestes (J. Pickering), W. Griffith, 1567.
T.F.T., 1910.
Brandl.

Impatient Poverty (anonymous), J. King, 1560.
T.F.T., 1907.
Bang, XXXIII, 1911.
J. S. Farmer, *'Lost' Tudor Plays*, 1907.

Jack Juggler (anonymous), W. Copland, n.d. (1562?).
M.S.R., 1933 (also, M.S.R. 1937, J. Allde's edn., n.d.).
T.F.T., 1912.
W. H. Williams, 1914.
Hazlitt's Dodsley, II.
J. S. Farmer, *Anonymous Plays*, series 3, 1907.

Jacob and Esau (anonymous), H. Bynneman, 1568.
T.F.T., 1908.
M.S.R., 1956.
Hazlitt's Dodsley, II.
J. S. Farmer, *Six Anonymous Plays*, series 2, 1906.

John the Baptist (J. Bale), Edition, now lost, without printer's name or date (1538?).
H. Ellis, *Harleian Miscellany* (1808), I, 101–14.

John the Evangelist (anonymous), J. Waley, n.d. (before 1557?).
T.F.T., 1907.
M.S.R., 1907.
J. S. Farmer, *'Lost' Tudor Plays*, 1907.

Johan Johan, Tyb his Wife, and Sir Johan (J. Heywood), W. Rastell, 1533.
T.F.T., 1907.
Brandl.
Gayley, I.
Adams.

King Darius (anonymous), T. Colwell, 1565.
T.F.T., 1909 (also, T.F.T. 1907, the edition of 1577).
Brandl.
J. S. Farmer, *Anonymous Plays*, series 3, 1906.

King John (J. Bale), MS.
M.S.R., 1931.
Bang, XXV, 1909.
Manly, I.

Liberality and Prodigality (anonymous: S. Westcott?), S. Stafford, 1602.
T.F.T., 1912.
M.S.R., 1913.
Hazlitt's Dodsley, VIII.

Like will to Like (U. Fulwell), E. Allde, 1587 (first printed by J. Allde, 1568).
T.F.T., 1909.
Hazlitt's Dodsley, III.

The longer thou livest, the more Fool thou art (W. Wager), W. How for R. Jhones, n.d. (1569).
T.F.T., 1910.
A. Brandl, *Shakespeare Jahrbuch*, XXXVI, 1900.

Love (J. Heywood), W. Rastell, 1534.
T.F.T., 1909 (J. Waley's edn., n.d.).
Brandl.
K. W. Cameron, 1944.

Love feigned and unfeigned (anonymous), MS.
M.S.R., *Collections*, I. i (1907).

Lusty Juventus (R. Wever), J. Awdeley, n.d. (1570?) (previous editions by W. Copland and A. Veale, n.d., both 1565?).
T.F.T., 1907.
Hazlitt's Dodsley, II.
J. S. Farmer, *Dramatic Writings of Richard Wever and Thomas Ingelend*, 1905.

Magnificence (J. Skelton), J. Rastell, n.d. (by 1533).
T.F.T., 1910.
R. L. Ramsay, E.E.T.S. 1906.

Mankind (anonymous), MS.
F. J. Furnivall and A. W. Pollard, *The Macro Plays*, E.E.T.S. 1904.

The Marriage of Wit and Science (anonymous), T. Marshe, n.d.
T.F.T., 1909.
Hazlitt's Dodsley, II.

The Marriage of Wit and Wisdom (anonymous), MS. dated 1579.
T.F.T., 1909.
J. O. Halliwell, Shakespeare Society, 1846.

Mary Magdalene (L. Wager), J. Charlewood, 1566.
F. I. Carpenter, Chicago, 1904.
T.F.T., 1908 (Charlewood's 1567 edition).

Misogonus (anonymous), MS. dated 1577.
R. W. Bond, *Early Plays from the Italian*, 1911.
Brandl.
J. S. Farmer, *Six Anonymous Plays*, series 2, 1906.

Mundus et Infans (anonymous), W. de Worde, 1522.
T.F.T., 1909.
Hazlitt's Dodsley, I.
Manly, I.

Nature (H. Medwall), J. Rastell? n.d. (1525?).
T.F.T., 1908.
Brandl.
Bang, XII, 1905.
J. S. Farmer, '*Lost*' *Tudor Plays*, 1907.

New Custom (anonymous), W. How for A. Veale, 1573.
T.F.T., 1908.
Hazlitt's Dodsley, III.
J. S. Farmer, *Anonymous Plays*, series 3, 1906.

Nice Wanton (anonymous), J. King, 1560.
T.F.T., 1909.
Hazlitt's Dodsley, II.
Manly, I.

The Pardoner and the Friar (J. Heywood), W. Rastell, 1533.
T.F.T., 1907.
Hazlitt's Dodsley, I.

Patient Grissell (J. Phillip), T. Colwell, n.d.
M.S.R., 1909.

The Pedlar's Prophecy (anonymous), T. Creede, sold by W. Barley, 1595.
T.F.T., 1911.
M.S.R., 1914.

Comedy of the Prodigal Son (anonymous, re-translated from the German version of a lost English play).
R. Simpson, *The School of Shakespeare*, II.

The Prodigal Son (anonymous), fragment, n.d. (1530?).
M.S.R., *Collections*, I. i (1907).

Roister Doister (N. Udall), H. Denham for T. Hackett? 1566? (copy imperfect).
M.S.R., 1934 (1935).
Hazlitt's Dodsley, III.
Manly, II.
Gayley, I.
Adams.
Numerous other editions.

Respublica (anonymous), MS.
W. W. Greg, E.E.T.S., 1952.
L. A. Magnus, E.E.T.S., 1905.
T.F.T., 1908.
Brandl.
J. S. Farmer, *'Lost' Tudor Plays*, 1907.

Ane Satyre of the Thrie Estaitis (Sir D. Lyndsay), R. Charteris, 1602.
D. Hamer, *Works of Sir David Lindsay*, II (1931).

Somebody, Avarice and Minister (anonymous), fragment, n.d. (1550?).
M.S.R., *Collections*, II. iii (1931).

Susanna (T. Garter), H. Jackson, 1578.
M.S.R., 1936 (1937).

Temperance and Humility (anonymous), fragment, n.d. (1537?).
M.S.R., *Collections*, I.iii (1909).

The Temptation of Our Lord (J. Bale), D. van den Straten? Wesel? n.d. (1547–48?).
T.F.T., 1909.

Thersites (anonymous), J. Tysdale, n.d. (1560?).
T.F.T., 1912.
Hazlitt's Dodsley, I.
J. S. Farmer, *Six Anonymous Plays*, 1905.

Three Ladies of London (R. W[ilson]), R. Warde, 1584 (another, variant, edition 1592).
T.F.T., 1911.
Hazlitt's Dodsley, VI.

Three Laws (J. Bale), "Nicholas Bamburgensis, 1538."
T.F.T., 1908.
A. Schroeer, *Anglia*, V (1882).

Three Lords and Three Ladies of London (R. W[ilson]), R. Jones, 1590.
T.F.T., 1912.
Hazlitt's Dodsley, VI.

The Tide tarrieth No Man (G. Wapull), H. Jackson, 1576.
T.F.T., 1910.
E. Ruhl, *Shakespeare Jahrbuch*, XLIII, 1907.

Tom Tyler and his Wife (anonymous), F. Kirkman? 1661.
T.F.T., 1912.
M.S.R., 1910.
F. E. Schelling, *P.M.L.A.*, XV (1900).
J. S. Farmer, *Six Anonymous Plays*, series 2, 1906.

The Trial of Treasure (anonymous: W. Wager?), Thomas Purfoot, 1567.
T.F.T., 1908.
Hazlitt's Dodsley, III.
J. S. Farmer, *Anonymous Plays*, series 3, 1906.

Wealth and Health (anonymous), no publisher's name, or date (1558?).
M.S.R., 1907.
J. S. Farmer, '*Lost*' *Tudor Plays*, 1907.

The Weather (J. Heywood), J. Awdeley, n.d. (previous edition by W. Rastell, 1533).
T.F.T., 1909. (T.F.T. 1908, Rastell's edition.)
Brandl.

Wisdom (*Mind, Will and Understanding*) (anonymous), MS.
F. J. Furnivall and A. W. Pollard, *The Macro Plays*, E.E.T.S., 1904.

Wit and Science (J. Redford), MS.
M.S.R., 1951.
Adams.

Witty and Witless (J. Heywood), MS.
T.F.T., 1909.

Youth (anonymous), J. Waley (1557?) (previous edition by W. de Worde(?), n.d. (1520?)). W. Copland, n.d. (1562?).
T.F.T., 1909. (Waley's edition.)
Hazlitt's Dodsley, II.

Other Works.

ADAMS, Joseph Q. (editor), *Chief Pre-Shakespearian Dramas*, 1925.
ALBRIGHT, Victor E., *The Shakespearian Stage*, 1912.

BANG, W. (general editor), *Materialen zur Kunde des alteren englischen Dramas*. 1902–.
BARLOW, Jerome. See ROY, William.
BASKERVILL, C. R., *The Elizabethan Jig, and related song drama*, 1929.
BASKERVILL, C. R., "John Rastell's dramatic activities," *M.P.*, XIII (1915–16).
BATMAN, Stephen, *A christall glasse of Christian reformation, wherein the godly maye beholde the coloured abuses vsed in this our present tyme*, 1569.
BATMAN, Stephen, *The new arival of the three Gracis into Anglia*, 1573.
BATMAN, Stephen, [S.B.], *The trauayled pylgrime, bringing newes from all partes of the worlde*, 1569.
BOAS, F. S., *University Drama in the Tudor Age*, 1914.
BOND, R. W. (editor), *Early Plays from the Italian*, 1911.
BRADBROOK, M. C., *Themes and Conventions of Elizabethan Tragedy*, 1935.
BRANDL, Alois, *Quellen des weltlichen Dramas in England vor Shakespeare* in *Quellen und Forschungen zur Sprach- und Culturgeschichte der germanischen Volker*, LXXX, 1898.
BROOKE, C. F. T. (editor), *The Shakespeare Apocrypha*, 1908.
BROOKE, C. F. T., *The Tudor Drama*, 1912.

CAMERON, K. W., *John Heywood's "Play of the Wether" [sic], a study in early Tudor Drama*, 1941.
CHAMBERS, E. K., *The Elizabethan Stage*, 4 vols., 1923.

CHAMBERS, E. K., *The Mediaeval Stage*, 2 vols., 1903.
CHAMBERS, E. K., *William Shakespeare*, 2 vols., 1930.
CHAUCER, Geoffrey, *Works*, ed. F. N. Robinson, 1933.
CHESTER PLAYS, ed. H. Deimling (E.E.T.S.), 1893.
COHEN, Gustave, *Histoire de la mise en scène dans le théâtre religieux français du moyen âge*, 1906.
COLLIER, J. Payne, *The History of English Dramatic Poetry to the time of Shakespeare: and annals of the stage to the Restoration*, 3 vols., 2nd edition, 1879.
CRAIG, H. (editor), *Two Coventry Corpus Christi Plays* (E.E.T.S.), 1902.
CRAIK, T. W., "Some notes on Thomas Lupton's *All For Money*," *N. & Q.*, June 1954.
CRAIK, T. W., "The political interpretation of two Tudor interludes: *Temperance and Humility* and *Wealth and Health*," *R.E.S.*, IV (new series), 1953.
CRAIK, T. W., "The true source of John Heywood's *Johan Johan*," *M.L.R.*, XLV, 1950.
CUSHMAN, L. W., *The Devil and the Vice in the English Dramatic Literature before Shakespeare*, 1900.

DEKKER, Thomas, *Dramatic Works*, ed. R. H. Shepherd, 4 vols., 1873.
DIGBY PLAYS, ed. F. J. Furnivall, (E.E.T.S.), 1896.
DODGSON, Campbell, *Catalogue of Early German and Flemish Woodcuts, British Museum*, Vol. 1., 1903.
DODSLEY, R. (original editor), *A Select Collection of Old Plays*, 4th edn., by W. C. Hazlitt, 15 vols., 1874–76.
DOWNER, A. S., *The British Drama: a handbook and brief chronicle*, 1950.

ELLIS, H. (editor), *The Harleian Miscellany*, 11 vols., 1808.
ERASMUS, Desiderius, *All the Familiar Colloquies of Erasmus*, N. Bailey's translation, 1733.

FARMER, J. S. (editor), "*Lost*" *Tudor Plays, with some others*, 1907.
FARNHAM, Willard, *The Medieval Heritage of Elizabethan Tragedy*, 1956.
FEUILLERAT, A., *Documents relating to the Revels at Court in the time of King Edward VI and Queen Mary*, (the Losely MSS.), Bang, *Materialen*, 44, 1914.
FEUILLERAT, A., *Documents relating to the Office of the Revels in the time of Queen Elizabeth*, Bang, *Materialen*, 21, 1908.
FOXE, John, *Actes and Monuments*, ed. S. R. Cattley, 8 vols., 1838.
FROUDE, J. A., *Life and Letters of Erasmus*, 1916.

GEISBERG, Max, *Der Deutsche Einblatt-Holzschnitt*, 1930.
GOTCH, J. A., *The Growth of the English House*, 2nd edn. enlarged, 1928.

HALL, Edward, *Chronicle* (*The Union of the Two Noble and Illustre Famelies York and Lancaster*), ed. H. Ellis, 1809.
HAMER, D. (editor), *The Works of Sir David Lindsay of the Mount*, (S.T.S.), 4 vols., 1931–36.
HARBAGE, A., *Annals of English Drama, 975–1700*, 1940.
HARRIS, Jesse W., *John Bale* (*Illinois Studies in Language and Literature*, 25, iv), 1940.
HOTSON, Leslie, *Shakespeare's Motley*, 1952.

JONSON, Ben, *Works*, ed. C. H. Herford and Percy and Evelyn Simpson, 1925–52.

KERNODLE, G. R., *From Art to Theatre: form and convention in the Renaissance*, 1944.

LATIMER, Hugh, *Sermons*, ed. G. E. Corrie (Parker Society), 1844.
LAWRENCE, W. J., *Pre-Restoration Stage Studies*, 1927.
LINTILHAC, E., *La comédie, moyen âge et renaissance*, (Vol. II of his *Histoire générale du théâtre en France*), n.d. (1906?)
LUDUS COVENTRIAE, ed. K. S. Block (E.E.T.S.), 1922.
LUPTON, Thomas, *A Dreame of the Deuill and Diues*, 1615.
LYLY, John, *The Complete Works*, ed. R. W. Bond, 3 vols., 1902.

McCUSKER, H. C., *John Bale, dramatist and antiquary*, 1942.
MACHYN, Henry, *Diary, 1550–63*, ed. J. G. Nichols (Camden Society), 1848.
MALONE SOCIETY REPRINTS, General Editor W. W. Greg, 1907–.
MARLE, R. van, *Iconographie de l'art profane au moyen âge et à la Renaissance, et la décoration des demeures*, 1931.
MARLOWE, Christopher, *Works*, ed. C. F. Tucker Brooke, 1910.
MILL, Anna J., *Medieval plays in Scotland*, 1927.
MILL, Anna J., "Representations of Lyndsay's *Satyre of the Thrie Estaitis*," *P.M.L.A.*, XLVII, 1932.
MORE, Thomas, *The workes of Sir T. More, wrytten by him in the Englishe tonge*, 1557.
MOTTER, T. H. V., *The School Drama in England*, 1929.

NICHOLS, J., *The Progresses and public processions of Queen Elizabeth*, 3 vols., 1823.
NICHOLS, J., *The Progresses, processions and magnificent festivities of King James the First*, 4 vols., 1828.
NICOLL, Allardyce, *British Drama*, 4th edn. revised, 1947.
NICOLL, Allardyce, *The Development of the Theatre*, 3rd edn. revised, 1948.

OLIVER, L. M., "John Foxe and the drama *New Custom*," *H.L.Q.*, August 1947.
OLIVER, L. M., "William Wager and *The Trial of Treasure*," *H.L.Q.*, August 1946.

PERCY, T. (editor), *Reliques of Ancient English Poetry*, Everyman's Library, 2 vols., n.d.
POLLARD, A. W. (editor), *Fifteenth Century Prose and Verse*, 1903.

RABELAIS, François, *Gargantua* and *Pantagruel*, translated by Urquhart and Motteux, Everyman's Library, 2 vols., n.d.
RAMSAY, R. L. (editor), Skelton's *Magnificence*, (E.E.T.S.), 1906.
REED, A. W., *Early Tudor Drama*, 1926.
REYHER, P., *Les masques anglais*, 1909.
ROBINSON, R., *The rewarde of wickednesse*, 1574.
ROSSITER, A. P., *English Drama from early times to the Elizabethans*, 1950.
ROY, William and BARLOW, Jerome, *Rede me and be nott wrothe*, ed. E. Arber, (Arber's English Reprints, XIV), 1871.

SHAKESPEARE, William, *Comedies, Histories, and Tragedies*, 1623.
SHARP, T., *A dissertation on the pageants or dramatic mysteries anciently performed at Coventry, by the trading companies of that city*, 1825.
SKELTON, John, *Poetical Works*, ed. A. Dyce, 2 vols., 1843.
SMITH, G. C. Moore (editor), "The Academic Drama at Cambridge: Extracts from College Records," Malone Society, *Collections*, II. ii, 1923.
SPENSER, Edmund, *Works*, ed. R. Morris (Globe edition), 1869.
SYMONDS, J. A., *Shakespere's predecessors in the English Drama*, 2nd. edn., 1900.

TIPPING, H. A., *English Homes*, 1920.
TUDOR FACSIMILE TEXTS, Editor J. S. Farmer, 1907–14.
TYNDALE, William, *The whole works of W. Tyndall, J. Frith and Doct. Barnes*, 2 vols., 1573, 1572.

WATERHOUSE, O. (editor), *The Non-Cycle Mystery Plays*, (E.E.T.S.), 1909.
WEBSTER, John, *Works*, ed. F. L. Lucas, 4 vols., 1927.
WELSFORD, E., *The Court Masque: a study in the relationship between poetry and the revels*, 1927.
WILLIS, R. and CLARK, J. W., *The Architectural History of the University of Cambridge*, 4 vols., 1886.
WINKLER, F. (editor), *Klassiker der Kunst: Dürer*.
WRIGHT, C. T., "Some Conventions regarding the Usurer in Elizabethan Literature," *S.P.*, XXXI, (1934).

INDEX